PARADE OF LIFE

Anthea Maton
Former NSTA National Coordinator
Project Scope, Sequence, Coordination
Washington, DC

Jean Hopkins
Science Instructor and Department Chairperson
John H. Wood Middle School
San Antonio, Texas

Susan Johnson
Professor of Biology
Ball State University
Muncie, Indiana

David LaHart
Senior Instructor
Florida Solar Energy Center
Cape Canaveral, Florida

Maryanna Quon Warner
Science Instructor
Del Dios Middle School
Escondido, California

Jill D. Wright
Professor of Science Education
Director of International Field Programs
University of Pittsburgh
Pittsburgh, Pennsylvania

Prentice Hall
Englewood Cliffs, New Jersey
Needham, Massachusetts

Prentice Hall Science

Parade of Life: Animals

Student Text and Annotated Teacher's Edition
Laboratory Manual
Teacher's Resource Package
Teacher's Desk Reference
Computer Test Bank
Teaching Transparencies
Product Testing Activities
Computer Courseware
Video and Interactive Video

The illustration on the cover, rendered by Joseph Cellini, depicts a herd of rhinos, which are among the endangered animals that live in Africa.

Credits begin on page 176.

SECOND EDITION

© 1994, 1993 by Prentice-Hall, Inc., Englewood Cliffs, New Jersey 07632.
All rights reserved. No part of this book may be reproduced in any form or by any means without permission in writing from the publisher. Printed in the United States of America.

ISBN 0-13-400433-7

3 4 5 6 7 8 9 10   97 96 95 94

Prentice Hall
A Division of Simon & Schuster
Englewood Cliffs, New Jersey 07632

STAFF CREDITS

Editorial:	Harry Bakalian, Pamela E. Hirschfeld, Maureen Grassi, Robert P. Letendre, Elisa Mui Eiger, Lorraine Smith-Phelan, Christine A. Caputo
Design:	AnnMarie Roselli, Carmela Pereira, Susan Walrath, Leslie Osher, Art Soares
Production:	Suse F. Bell, Joan McCulley, Elizabeth Torjussen, Christina Burghard
Photo Research:	Libby Forsyth, Emily Rose, Martha Conway
Publishing Technology:	Andrew Grey Bommarito, Deborah Jones, Monduane Harris, Michael Colucci, Gregory Myers, Cleasta Wilburn
Marketing:	Andrew Socha, Victoria Willows
Pre-Press Production:	Laura Sanderson, Kathryn Dix, Denise Herckenrath
Manufacturing:	Rhett Conklin, Gertrude Szyferblatt

Consultants

Kathy French	National Science Consultant
Jeannie Dennard	National Science Consultant
Brenda Underwood	National Science Consultant
Janelle Conarton	National Science Consultant

Contributing Writers

Linda Densman
Science Instructor
Hurst, TX

Linda Grant
Former Science Instructor
Weatherford, TX

Heather Hirschfeld
Science Writer
Durham, NC

Marcia Mungenast
Science Writer
Upper Montclair, NJ

Michael Ross
Science Writer
New York City, NY

Content Reviewers

Dan Anthony
Science Mentor
Rialto, CA

John Barrow
Science Instructor
Pomona, CA

Leslie Bettencourt
Science Instructor
Harrisville, RI

Carol Bishop
Science Instructor
Palm Desert, CA

Dan Bohan
Science Instructor
Palm Desert, CA

Steve M. Carlson
Science Instructor
Milwaukie, OR

Larry Flammer
Science Instructor
San Jose, CA

Steve Ferguson
Science Instructor
Lee's Summit, MO

Robin Lee Harris Freedman
Science Instructor
Fort Bragg, CA

Edith H. Gladden
Former Science Instructor
Philadelphia, PA

Vernita Marie Graves
Science Instructor
Tenafly, NJ

Jack Grube
Science Instructor
San Jose, CA

Emiel Hamberlin
Science Instructor
Chicago, IL

Dwight Kertzman
Science Instructor
Tulsa, OK

Judy Kirschbaum
Science/Computer Instructor
Tenafly, NJ

Kenneth L. Krause
Science Instructor
Milwaukie, OR

Ernest W. Kuehl, Jr.
Science Instructor
Bayside, NY

Mary Grace Lopez
Science Instructor
Corpus Christi, TX

Warren Maggard
Science Instructor
PeWee Valley, KY

Della M. McCaughan
Science Instructor
Biloxi, MS

Stanley J. Mulak
Former Science Instructor
Jensen Beach, FL

Richard Myers
Science Instructor
Portland, OR

Carol Nathanson
Science Mentor
Riverside, CA

Sylvia Neivert
Former Science Instructor
San Diego, CA

Jarvis VNC Pahl
Science Instructor
Rialto, CA

Arlene Sackman
Science Instructor
Tulare, CA

Christine Schumacher
Science Instructor
Pikesville, MD

Suzanne Steinke
Science Instructor
Towson, MD

Len Svinth
Science Instructor/ Chairperson
Petaluma, CA

Elaine M. Tadros
Science Instructor
Palm Desert, CA

Joyce K. Walsh
Science Instructor
Midlothian, VA

Steve Weinberg
Science Instructor
West Hartford, CT

Charlene West, PhD
Director of Curriculum
Rialto, CA

John Westwater
Science Instructor
Medford, MA

Glenna Wilkoff
Science Instructor
Chesterfield, OH

Edee Norman Wiziecki
Science Instructor
Urbana, IL

Teacher Advisory Panel

Beverly Brown
Science Instructor
Livonia, MI

James Burg
Science Instructor
Cincinnati, OH

Karen M. Cannon
Science Instructor
San Diego, CA

John Eby
Science Instructor
Richmond, CA

Elsie M. Jones
Science Instructor
Marietta, GA

Michael Pierre McKereghan
Science Instructor
Denver, CO

Donald C. Pace, Sr.
Science Instructor
Reisterstown, MD

Carlos Francisco Sainz
Science Instructor
National City, CA

William Reed
Science Instructor
Indianapolis, IN

Multicultural Consultant

Steven J. Rakow
Associate Professor
University of Houston— Clear Lake
Houston, TX

English as a Second Language (ESL) Consultants

Jaime Morales
Bilingual Coordinator
Huntington Park, CA

Pat Hollis Smith
Former ESL Instructor
Beaumont, TX

Reading Consultant

Larry Swinburne
Director
Swinburne Readability Laboratory

CONTENTS

PARADE OF LIFE: ANIMALS

Activity Bank/Reference Section

Features

CONCEPT MAPPING

Throughout your study of science, you will learn a variety of terms, facts, figures, and concepts. Each new topic you encounter will provide its own collection of words and ideas—which, at times, you may think seem endless. But each of the ideas within a particular topic is related in some way to the others. No concept in science is isolated. Thus it will help you to understand the topic if you see the whole picture; that is, the interconnectedness of all the individual terms and ideas. This is a much more effective and satisfying way of learning than memorizing separate facts.

Actually, this should be a rather familiar process for you. Although you may not think about it in this way, you analyze many of the elements in your daily life by looking for relationships or connections. For example, when you look at a collection of flowers, you may divide them into groups: roses, carnations, and daisies. You may then associate colors with these flowers: red, pink, and white. The general topic is flowers. The subtopic is types of flowers. And the colors are specific terms that describe flowers. A topic makes more sense and is more easily understood if you understand how it is broken down into individual ideas and how these ideas are related to one another and to the entire topic.

It is often helpful to organize information visually so that you can see how it all fits together. One technique for describing related ideas is called a **concept map**. In a concept map, an idea is represented by a word or phrase enclosed in a box. There are several ideas in any concept map. A connection between two ideas is made with a line. A word or two that describes the connection is written on or near the line. The general topic is located at the top of the map. That topic is then broken down into subtopics, or more specific ideas, by branching lines. The most specific topics are located at the bottom of the map.

To construct a concept map, first identify the important ideas or key terms in the chapter or section. Do not try to include too much information. Use your judgment as to what is really important. Write the general topic at the top of your map. Let's use an example to help illustrate this process. Suppose you decide that the key terms in a section you are reading are School, Living Things, Language Arts, Subtraction, Grammar, Mathematics, Experiments, Papers, Science, Addition, Novels. The general topic is School. Write and enclose this word in a box at the top of your map.

SCHOOL

Now choose the subtopics—Language Arts, Science, Mathematics. Figure out how they are related to the topic. Add these words to your map. Continue this procedure until you have included all the important ideas and terms. Then use lines to make the appropriate connections between ideas and terms. Don't forget to write a word or two on or near the connecting line to describe the nature of the connection.

Do not be concerned if you have to redraw your map (perhaps several times!) before you show all the important connections clearly. If, for example, you write papers for Science as well as for Language Arts, you may want to place these two subjects next to each other so that the lines do not overlap.

One more thing you should know about concept mapping: Concepts can be correctly mapped in many different ways. In fact, it is unlikely that any two people will draw identical concept maps for a complex topic. Thus there is no one correct concept map for any topic! Even though your concept map may not match those of your classmates, it will be correct as long as it shows the most important concepts and the clear relationships among them. Your concept map will also be correct if it has meaning to you and if it helps you understand the material you are reading. A concept map should be so clear that if some of the terms are erased, the missing terms could easily be filled in by following the logic of the concept map.

PARADE OF LIFE
Animals

Everyone loves a friendly animal—the cricket that warms itself by a campfire, the frog that "sings" on a rock in a pond, the first robin to alight on your lawn in the spring, the squirrel that "plants" acorns from your oak tree, or the porpoise that frolics near a boat full of people. These creatures delight us because, unlike most animals, they seem not to be frightened by us.

However, there are animals that scurry away at the mere sound, smell, or sight of humans. Deer, for example, rapidly flee when they hear or smell an intruder. Cottontails use their hind legs to run when their large ears hear approaching danger. When frightened by our presence, an octopus emits an inky cloud to make good its escape!

Other animals—such as termites, flies, rats, mosquitoes, cockroaches, and hookworms—are regarded as pests. These animals cost us millions of dollars annually in damage to property and health. Still other animals are seen as terrifying menaces: the great white sharks, rattlesnakes, lions, tigers, and wolves.

Invertebrates, or animals without backbones, inhabit the Earth's land, sea, and air. The sponge (top) and the insect (right) are two examples of invertebrates.

CHAPTERS

The wolf (left) belongs to a group of vertebrates, or animals with backbones, known as mammals. Like the wolf, the iguana (bottom) is a vertebrate. It belongs to a group of animals known as reptiles.

Whatever their behavior toward us, each of these animals has a specific role in nature. As you read this textbook, you will discover a great deal about the animals that inhabit the Earth's lands, water, and air. So read on and discover why the Earth is referred to as the living planet.

Discovery *Activity*

Animals, Animals

1. Take a look at a small area near your home. The area can be located in a park, an empty lot, a yard, or on a beach.

2. Make a list of all the animals you observe in the area. Make a sketch of each animal.

   ■ What are the characteristics of the animals you observed?

   ■ Which animals have similar characteristics? Which have different characteristics?

   ■ If you could develop your own system of classification, how would you group each animal on your list?

Sponges, Cnidarians, Worms, and *Mollusks*

Guide for Reading

After you read the following sections, you will be able to

1-1 The Five Kingdoms
- ■ Describe the five kingdoms of living things.

1-2 Introduction to the Animal Kingdom
- ■ Compare vertebrates and invertebrates.

1-3 Sponges
- ■ Describe the characteristics of sponges.

1-4 Cnidarians
- ■ Describe the characteristics of cnidarians.

1-5 Worms
- ■ Compare flatworms, roundworms, and segmented worms.

1-6 Mollusks
- ■ Identify three groups of mollusks.

No other beast of the sea has been as feared as the octopus. Its very name—devilfish—calls to mind danger and alarm. Yet the truth is that the octopus would be more afraid of you than you should be of it. The octopus, you see, is terrified of anything larger than itself.

Of the hundred or so varieties of octopuses, most grow no larger than one meter across. Some are so tiny that they could sit on your fingernail! In the Mediterranean Sea, where octopuses are common, very few grow tentacles that reach two meters in length. Only in the depths of the Pacific Ocean are there believed to be really tremendous octopuses.

No matter what their actual size, the tales told about octopuses were common among people with vivid imaginations. In such stories, octopuses attacked ships, slung their tentacled arms around the masts, and nearly capsized the vessels. Actually, few scientists believe that octopuses intentionally attack humans.

Octopuses are one of many fascinating animals you will read about in this textbook. In this chapter you will begin to explore this marvelous world by examining sponges, cnidarians, worms, and mollusks.

Journal *Activity*

You and Your World In your journal, write down five common expressions that have to do with animals. Here are two examples: ''At a snail's pace'' and ''It's a fluke.'' Next to each expression, explain its meaning as you understand it. When you have finished reading this textbook, look again at your list. See if you can explain the origin of each expression.

◄ *An octopus resting on its tentacles*

Activity Bank

To Classify or Not to Classify?, p.152

Figure 1–1 *The many different types of environments in which organisms live include tropical rain forests and ocean depths.*

1–1 The Five Kingdoms

Just by looking around you, you can see that you share the Earth with many different types of organisms, or living things. Insects, cows, horses, trees, flowers, grasses, bacteria, mushrooms, and fishes are but a few examples. But what you may not know is that scientists have already identified more than 2.5 million species, or groups of organisms that share similar characteristics and that can breed with one another. What is even more amazing is that the job is far from over! In fact, some scientists estimate that there may be millions more organisms living in areas such as the tropical rain forests and the lower depths of the Earth's oceans that have not as yet been identified.

To help study all known species, which is an impossible task at best, scientists have divided all life on Earth into several **kingdoms,** or large, general groups. **Today, the most generally accepted system of classification contains five kingdoms: monerans** (MOHN-er-ans), **protists** (PROHT-ihsts), **fungi** (FUHN-jigh; singular: fungus), **plants, and animals.**

As is often the case in science, not all scientists agree on this classification system. And their disagreement is important for you to keep in mind. Someday, research may show that different classification systems make more sense and better describe how living things have evolved (changed). But for now, this five-kingdom classification system is a useful way to study living things.

MONERANS All the Earth's bacteria are members of the kingdom Monera. Monerans are unicellular organisms, or organisms that are made of one cell. The cell of a moneran does not contain a nucleus, which is the control center of a cell. A moneran's cell, in fact, does not have many of the structures found in other cells. This fact has led scientists to believe that monerans are distant relatives of the other four kingdoms.

Like other organisms, monerans can be placed into two divisions, based on how they get their energy. Organisms that obtain their energy by making their own food are called **autotrophs** (AW-toh-trohfs). Organisms that cannot make their own food

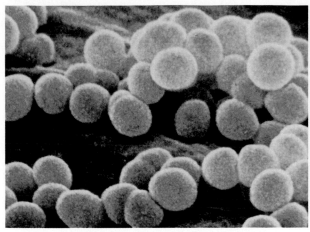
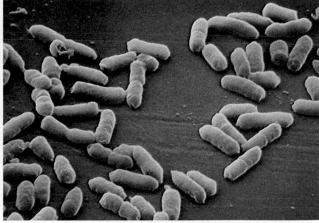

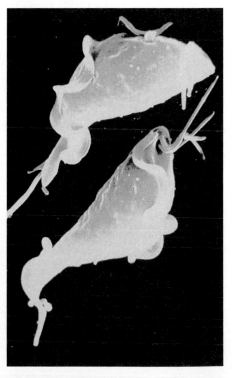

are called **heterotrophs** (HEHT-er-oh-trohfs). Heterotrophs may eat autotrophs in order to obtain food. Or they may eat other heterotrophs. Whatever the case, all heterotrophs rely on autotrophs for food.

Scientists have evidence that monerans first appeared on Earth about 3.5 billion years ago. (Remember, the Earth is estimated to be more than 4 billion years old.) This makes monerans the earliest life forms on Earth.

PROTISTS The kingdom Protista contains most of the unicellular organisms that have a nucleus. In addition to a nucleus, protists also have special cell structures that perform specific functions.

Some protists move like animals but at the same time have several obvious plantlike characteristics. Specifically, they are green in color and can use light energy to make their own food from simple substances.

Protists were the first living things to contain a nucleus. Ancient types of protists that lived millions of years ago are probably the ancestors of modern protists, fungi, plants, and animals.

FUNGI Fungi make up the kingdom Fungi. Most fungi are multicellular organisms, or organisms that are made of many cells. Although you may not realize it, you are probably quite familiar with fungi. Mushrooms are fungi. So are the molds that sometimes grow on leftover food that has stayed too long in the refrigerator. And the mildews that form small black spots in damp bathrooms and basements are also fungi.

Figure 1–2 *These spherical-shaped bacteria and rod-shaped bacteria are placed in the kingdom Monera. What are the characteristics of monerans?*

Figure 1–3 *The kingdom Protista contains most of the unicellular organisms that have a nucleus. Examples of protists include Trichomonas.*

Figure 1–4 *The red mushroom is a fungus. Can you name other examples of fungi?*

Until a short time ago, fungi were classified as plants. However, fungi differ from plants in several basic ways. The most obvious difference between plants and fungi is that plants are able to use light energy to make their own food from simple substances. Fungi are not. Fungi, like animals, must obtain their energy from another source.

PLANTS As you might expect, plants make up the kingdom Plantae. Most members of the plant kingdom are multicellular organisms. The members of this kingdom that are probably most familiar to you are flowering plants, trees, mosses, ferns, and some algae.

ANIMALS Animals are the multicellular organisms that make up the kingdom Animalia. Animals have specialized tissues, and most have organs and organ systems. Because animals cannot make their own food, they are heterotrophs. And, unlike plant cells, animal cells do not have cell walls.

Figure 1–5 *The two kingdoms of organisms that you are probably most familiar with are the plants and the animals. Most plants, such as the trees and mosses on this forest floor, are multicellular (left). However, there are some plants that are unicellular. All animals, such as the hippopotamus (center) and the helmeted lizard (right), are multicellular organisms.*

1-1 Section Review

1. What are the five kingdoms of living things?
2. List two important characteristics of each kingdom.
3. How does an autotroph obtain its food? A heterotroph?

Critical Thinking—*Applying Concepts*
4. Suppose a new species is found to be a multicellular heterotroph whose cells lack cell walls. To which kingdom of organisms would this species belong? Explain.

1-2 Introduction to the Animal Kingdom

Think of a fierce lion, a friendly porpoise, a cuddly puppy, a crawling earthworm, an annoying mosquito, and a slimy jellyfish. Now ask yourself what all these organisms have in common. You are correct if you say they are all animals and belong to the kingdom Animalia. As you have just learned, animals can be defined as multicellular heterotrophs whose cells lack cell walls.

Animal cells vary greatly in size. Although most cells are too small to be seen without a microscope, some cells are large enough to be seen with the unaided eye. The largest animal cell is the yolk of an ostrich egg. This yolk, or single cell, is about the size of a baseball. Animal cells also have different shapes. Some are shaped like long rectangles, some like spheres, some like disks. Others are rod shaped or spiral shaped.

In most animals, cells are organized into tissues, tissues into organs, and organs into organ systems. Every kind of cell depends on every other kind of cell for its survival and for the survival of the entire animal.

The animal kingdom can be grouped into two major divisions: **vertebrates** and **invertebrates.**

Guide for Reading

Focus on this question as you read.

▶ *What is the difference between a vertebrate and an invertebrate?*

ACTIVITY

WRITING

Symmetry

The body shapes of invertebrates show either radial symmetry, bilateral symmetry, or asymmetry. Use a science dictionary or science encyclopedia to define each term.

Make a list of the different phyla of invertebrates discussed in this chapter. Indicate what type of symmetry is shown by each phylum.

Figure 1–6 *All members of the kingdom Animalia can be grouped into two major divisions: vertebrates and invertebrates. Warthogs (top left) and dusky dolphins (top right) are vertebrates; sea stars (bottom left) and tarantulas (bottom right) are invertebrates. How can you distinguish between a vertebrate and an invertebrate?*

Friends or Foes?, p.153

Humans, lions, porpoises, and puppies are all examples of vertebrates. **A vertebrate is an animal that has a backbone, or vertebral** (VER-tuh-bruhl) **column.** Earthworms, mosquitoes, and jellyfishes are all invertebrates. **An invertebrate is an animal that has no backbone.** Invertebrates make up about 90 percent of all animal species.

All animals in the kingdom Animalia are divided into different groups called phyla (FIGH-luh; singular: phylum) according to their body structure. A phylum is the second largest group of organisms after kingdom. As you explore the invertebrate phyla, keep in mind that they share an evolutionary heritage. In

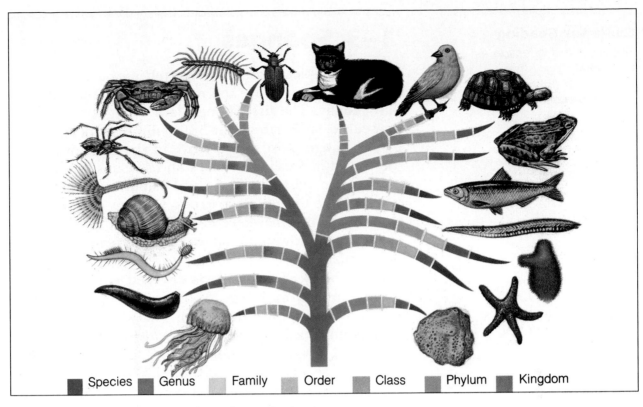

| | Species | | Genus | | Family | | Order | | Class | | Phylum | | Kingdom |

Figure 1–7 *The evolutionary tree shows the best understanding of the evolutionary relationships between different groups of organisms. Which invertebrates seem to be most closely related to vertebrates?*

other words, the invertebrates (as well as all animals) share a common ancestor. This fact will become evident to you as you move from one animal phylum to another.

1–2 Section Review

1. What is an animal?
2. How are vertebrates and invertebrates alike? How are they different?
3. What is a phylum? Would you expect to find more species in a phylum or a kingdom? Explain.

Critical Thinking—*Drawing Conclusions*
4. Why do multicellular organisms need specialized tissues?

1–3 Sponges

The simplest group of invertebrates are the sponges. Sponges are the most ancient of all animals alive today. The first sponges are thought to have appeared on Earth about 580 million years ago.

Although most sponges live in the sea, some can be found in freshwater lakes and streams. Sponges grow attached to one spot and usually stay there for their entire life unless a strong wave or current washes them somewhere else. Because they show little or no movement, sponges were once thought to be plants.

The body of a sponge is covered with many pores, or tiny openings. Sponges belong to the phylum Porifera (poh-RIHF-er-uh). The word porifera means pore-bearers. Moving ocean water carries food and oxygen through the pores into the sponge. The sponge's cells remove food and oxygen from the water. At the same time, the cells release waste products (carbon dioxide and undigested food) into the water. Then, the water leaves through a larger opening.

Figure 1–8 *Sponges are invertebrates and belong to the phylum Porifera. As you can see from the photographs, sponges—such as* Callyspongia *sponges (left), tennis ball sponges (top), red sponges (bottom left), and Caribbean reef sponges (bottom right)—vary in shape, color, and size. What does the word porifera mean?*

Sponge cells are unusual in that they function on their own, without any coordination with one another. In fact, some people think of sponges as a colony of cells living together. Despite their independent functioning, however, sponge cells have a mysterious attraction to one another. This attraction can be easily demonstrated by passing a sponge through a fine filter so that it breaks into clumps of cells. Within hours, these cells reform into several new sponges. No other animal species shares this amazing ability of sponge cells to reorganize themselves.

Many sponges produce **spicules** (SPIHK-yoolz). Spicules are thin, spiny structures that form the skeleton of many sponges. Spicules are made of either a chalky or a glasslike substance. They interlock to form delicate skeletons, such as the one shown in Figure 1–11 on page 20. Other sponges have skeletons that consist of a softer, fiberlike material. The cleaned and dried skeletons of these sponges are the natural bath sponges that you may have in your home or see in department stores. Still other sponges have skeletons that are made of both spicules and the fiberlike material.

Sponges reproduce sexually and asexually. **Sexual reproduction** is the process by which a new organism forms from the joining of a female cell and a male cell. Reproducing sexually, one sponge produces eggs (female cells); another produces sperm

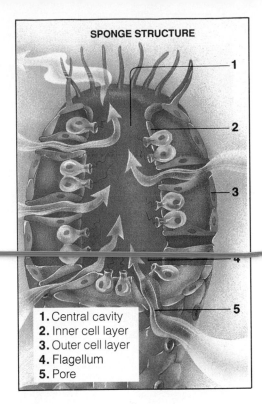

SPONGE STRUCTURE

1. Central cavity
2. Inner cell layer
3. Outer cell layer
4. Flagellum
5. Pore

Figure 1–9 *Notice that the body of a sponge consists of a layer of cells that form a wall around a central cavity. The cells in this layer function independently of one another.*

Figure 1–10 *In some sponges, such as the sponges in the photograph, eggs are squirted into the surrounding water, where they may be fertilized. In others, eggs are fertilized inside the body of the parent sponge.*

ACTIVITY
DISCOVERING

Observing a Sponge

1. Obtain a natural sponge from your teacher.

2. Use a hand lens to examine the surface and the pores. Draw what you see.

3. Remove a small piece of the sponge and place it on a glass microscope slide. Look for the spicules. Draw what you observe.

■ Repeat steps 2 and 3 with a synthetic kitchen sponge. How do a natural sponge and a synthetic sponge compare?

Figure 1–11 *The lacy skeleton of this glass sponge consists of thousands of spicules made of glassy material. What is the function of spicules?*

(male cells). These cells join, and a young sponge develops. **Asexual reproduction** is the process by which a single organism produces a new organism. Sponges reproduce asexually by budding. In budding, part of a sponge simply falls off the parent sponge and begins to grow into a new sponge. During cold winters, some freshwater sponges produce structures that contain groups of cells surrounded by a hard, protective layer. When conditions become favorable again, these structures grow into new sponges.

In addition to being the source of natural sponges, sponges are also an important source of powerful antibiotics that can be used to fight disease-causing bacteria and fungi. Sponges also provide homes and food for certain worms, shrimps, and starfishes.

1–3 Section Review

1. What are the main characteristics of sponges?
2. How do food and oxygen enter a sponge's body?
3. How do sponges reproduce?

Critical Thinking—*Making Predictions*
4. Predict what would happen to a sponge if it lived in water that contained a great deal of floating matter.

Guide for Reading

Focus on this question as you read.

▶ What are the main characteristics of cnidarians?

1–4 Cnidarians

The phylum Cnidaria (nigh-DAIR-ee-uh) consists of many invertebrate animals with dazzling colors and strange shapes. The animals that make up this phylum include corals, jellyfishes, hydras, and sea anemones. As you can see in Figure 1–12, cnidarians have two basic body forms: a vase-shaped polyp (PAHL-ihp) and a bowl-shaped medusa (muh-DOO-suh). A polyp usually remains in one place; a medusa can move from place to place.

Cnidarians have a hollow central cavity with only one opening called the mouth. The phylum

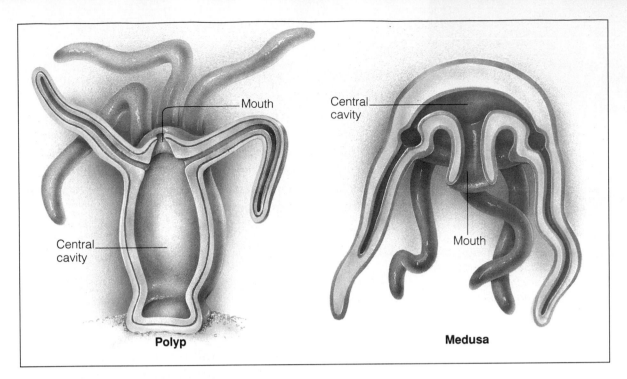

Figure 1–12 *Cnidarians have two basic body forms: a vase-shaped polyp and a bowl-shaped medusa. What is the difference between a polyp and a medusa?*

name Cnidaria is taken from the Greek word meaning to sting. All cnidarians have **nematocysts,** which are special stinging structures. Nematocysts are used to stun or kill a cnidarian's prey. It is no surprise then that nematocysts are found on the tentacles surrounding a cnidarian's mouth. After capturing and stunning its prey, a cnidarian pulls the prey into its mouth with the tentacles. Once the food is digested within its central cavity, a cnidarian releases waste products through its only opening, which is its mouth.

Unlike sponges, cnidarians contain groups of cells that perform special functions. In other words, cnidarians have specialized tissues. An example of a specialized tissue is a nerve net, which is a simple nervous system that is concentrated around a cnidarian's mouth but spreads throughout the body. An interesting characteristic of cnidarians can be seen in Figure 1–13. Notice that a cnidarian is symmetrical. If you drew a line through the center of its body, both sides would be the same.

Most cnidarians can reproduce both sexually and asexually. Like sponges, cnidarians reproduce asexually by budding and sexually by producing eggs and sperm.

Figure 1–13 *Jellyfishes have a type of symmetry in which their body parts repeat around an imaginary line drawn through the center of their body. What other invertebrates have this type of symmetry?*

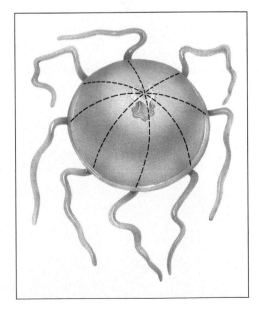

Figure 1-14 *Unlike most cnidarians, which live in salty oceans, these green hydras live in freshwater lakes and streams. How do hydras reproduce?*

Hydras

Hydras belong to a group of cnidarians that spend their lives as polyps (vase-shaped body forms). Hydras are the only cnidarians that live in fresh water. All other cnidarians live in salty oceans. Unlike most other types of polyps, hydras can move around with a somersaulting movement. They can reproduce either asexually by budding or sexually by producing eggs and sperm.

Corals

Like all cnidarians, corals are soft-bodied organisms. However, corals use minerals in the water to build hard, protective coverings of limestone. When a coral dies, the hard outer covering is left behind. Year after year, for many millions of years, generations of corals have lived and died, each generation adding a layer of limestone. In time, a coral reef forms. The Great Barrier Reef off the coast of Australia is an example of a coral reef. The top layer of the reef contains living corals. But underneath this "living stone" are the remains of corals that may have lived millions of years ago when dinosaurs walked the Earth.

Corals are polyps that live together in colonies. These colonies have a wide variety of shapes and

Figure 1-15 *Corals—such as staghorn corals (top left), lettuce corals (top right), grooved brain corals (bottom left), and tube corals (bottom right)—produce skeletons of calcium carbonate, or limestone.*

colors. Some coral colonies look like antlers. Others resemble fans swaying in the water. Still others resemble the structure of a human brain.

At first glance, a coral appears to be little more than a mouth surrounded by stinging tentacles. See Figure 1–15. But there is more to a coral than meets the eye. Living inside a coral's body are simple plant-like autotrophs known as algae. Algae help to make food for the coral. But because algae need sunlight to make food, corals must live in shallow water, where sunlight can reach them. The relationship between a coral animal and an alga plant is among the most unusual in nature.

CONNECTIONS

No Bones About It

What do coral and bone have in common? Until a few years ago, it was thought they had little in common. Today, however, there are more similarities between coral and bone than meet the eye. And these similarities have made coral an excellent stand-in for bones in repairing serious bone fractures, or breaks.

Because coral resembles bone, doctors have recently begun using it to replace bone. Before the coral is inserted into the body, however, it is heated. The heat changes limestone (calcium carbonate), which is the main substance in coral, into calcium-containing hydroxyapatite, which is the main ingredient in bone. In the process, living coral organisms are killed.

When the coral is placed at the site of the fracture, it blends almost seamlessly with the bone. The maze of channels within the coral provides passageways through which blood vessels from nearby bone can grow. A permanent bond between bone and coral results.

Over time, the coral becomes filled with new bone.

Because coral is made of material naturally found in bones, the body does not treat it as a foreign substance. In other words, coral does not seem to activate the body's immune system (the body's defense against foreign material) nor produce inflammation (a condition that causes redness, pain, and swelling). Thus the coral remains unaffected, and the body remains unharmed as new bone grows.

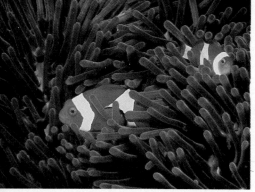

Figure 1–16 *The nematocysts on the tentacles of sea anemones are used to catch food. Although most large sea anemones eat fishes, this clownfish swims undisturbed through the sea anemone's tentacles. How do these two organisms help each other?*

Figure 1–17 *Jellyfishes, such as* Aequorea, *spend most of their life as bowl-shaped medusas.*

Sea Anemones

Can you see the fish swimming through what looks like a plant in Figure 1–16? That plant is actually an animal—a cnidarian known as a sea anemone (uh-NEHM-uh-nee). Sea anemones are polyps that resemble underwater flowers. Their "petals," however, are really tentacles that contain nematocysts (stinging structures). When a fish passes near a sea anemone's tentacles, the nematocysts stun the fish. Then the tentacles pull the fish into the sea anemone, where the stunned prey is digested within the central cavity.

If a fish is lucky enough to be a clownfish, however, it can swim unharmed through a sea anemone's tentacles. This friendly relationship between a sea anemone and a clownfish protects a clownfish from other fishes that might try to attack it. At the same time, a clownfish serves as living bait for a sea anemone. When other fishes see a clownfish swimming among a sea anemone's tentacles, they swim nearer, hoping to make the clownfish their next meal. But before they know it, they are grabbed by the sea anemone's tentacles and become its next meal!

Jellyfishes

If you have ever seen a jellylike cup floating in the ocean near you, you probably knew enough to stay clear of it. This cnidarian, known as a jellyfish, is one that most people recognize immediately.

Although a jellyfish may look harmless, it can deliver a painful poison through its nematocysts, which are located on its tentacles. In fact, even when the nematocysts are broken up into small pieces, they remain active. They can sting a passing swimmer who accidentally bumps into them. The largest jellyfish ever found had tentacles that reached out for more than 30 meters.

Of course, the nematocysts are not there merely to disturb unsuspecting swimmers. Like all cnidarians, jellyfishes use the nematocysts to capture prey. One type of jellyfish, the sea wasp jellyfish, produces a strong nerve poison that has helped scientists to better understand the function of nerves in humans.

1–4 Section Review

1. What is the main characteristic of cnidarians?
2. What is the function of nematocysts?
3. What is a polyp? A medusa?
4. What animals make up the phylum Cnidaria?

Critical Thinking—*Making Comparisons*

5. Which phylum is more complex—the sponges or the cnidarians? Explain your answer.

1–5 Worms

Most people think of worms as slimy, squiggly creatures. And, in fact, many are. There are, however, many kinds of worms that look nothing like the worms used to bait fishing hooks. You can see examples of such worms in Figure 1–18. Worms are classified into three main phyla based on their shapes. **The three phyla of worms are flatworms, roundworms, and segmented worms.**

If you were to draw an imaginary line down the entire length of a worm's body, you would discover that the right half is almost a mirror image of the left half. See Figure 1–19 on page 26. With the exception of one phylum, this body symmetry

Guide for Reading

Focus on these questions as you read.

▶ *What are the three main groups of worms?*

▶ *What are the characteristics of each group of worms?*

Figure 1–18 *Contrary to popular belief, many worms—such as the feather duster worm (left) and the sea mouse (right)—are neither squiggly nor are they slimy.*

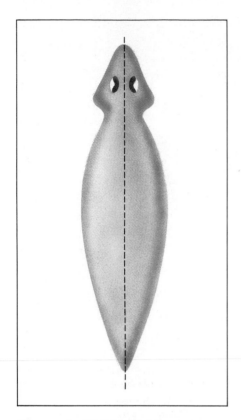

Figure 1–19 *Most of the more complex animals, such as the worms, have bodies in which the left half and the right half are almost mirror images of each other.*

Figure 1–20 *The planarian (right) is an example of a flatworm that is able to regenerate. An injury to this planarian (left) divided its head in half, and then the two halves regenerated their lost parts.*

(sameness of form on either side of a dividing line) is characteristic of all animals you will read about from here on, including worms.

Flatworms

Flatworms, as you might expect, have flat bodies. They are grouped in the phylum Platyhelminthes (plat-ih-hehl-MIHN-theez). The word platyhelminthes comes from two Greek words, *platy-*, meaning flat, and *helminth,* meaning worm. Some scientists believe that flatworms evolved from cnidarians. Other scientists are convinced that flatworms developed independently.

You have probably never seen a flatworm, much less a flatworm like the one in Figure 1–20. This flatworm is called a planarian. Most planarians, which are barely 0.5 centimeter long (a little less than the width of the nail on your pinky), live in ponds and streams—often on the underside of plant leaves or on underwater rocks. Planarians feed on dead plant or animal matter.

When there is little food available, however, some planarians do a rather unusual thing. They digest their own body parts. Later, when food is available once again, the missing parts regrow. Interestingly, if a planarian is cut into pieces, each piece eventually grows into a new planarian! The ability of an organism to regrow lost parts is called **regeneration.**

Some flatworms grow on or in living things and are called **parasites.** Tapeworms, which look like long, flat ribbons, live in the bodies of many animals, including humans. The head of a tapeworm has

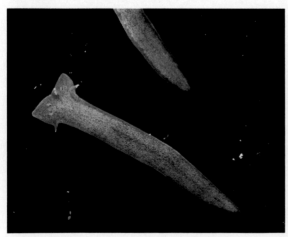

special hooks that are used to attach it to the tissues of a **host,** or the organism in which it lives. The tapeworm causes illness by taking a host's food and water, as well as by producing wastes and blocking the host's intestines.

A tapeworm can grow as long as 6 meters inside its host. However, size is not always a good indicator of danger. The most dangerous human tapeworm is only about 8 millimeters long and enters the body through microscopic eggs in some types of food.

Roundworms

You probably have been told never to eat pork unless it is well cooked. Do you know the reason for this warning? It has to do with a type of roundworm called *Trichinella* (trih-KIGH-nehl-uh), which lives in the muscle tissue of pigs. If a person eats a piece of raw or undercooked pork, *Trichinella* that are still alive in the pork enter the person's body. As many as 3000 roundworms can be contained in a single gram of raw or undercooked pork!

Once inside the body, the roundworms live and reproduce in the intestines of the host. Female roundworms release hundreds of immature round-worms, which are carried in the bloodstream. These immature roundworms then burrow into surrounding tissues and organs. This causes terrible pain for the host. Once inside tissues and organs, *Trichinella* become inactive. The name of this disease is trichi-nosis (trihk-ih-NOH-sihs).

Roundworms resemble strands of spaghetti with pointed ends. They belong to the phylum Nematoda (nehm-uh-TOHD-uh). The word nematode means threadlike. Roundworms live on land or in water. Many roundworms are animal parasites, although some live on plants. One type of roundworm, the hookworm, infects more than 600 million people in the world every year. Hookworms enter the body by burrowing through the skin on the soles of the feet. They eventually end up in the intestines of their hosts, where they live on the blood.

Figure 1–21 *Some flatworms, such as the tapeworm, are parasites. Notice that the head of a tapeworm has suckers and other structures that enable it to attach to the inside of its host's intestines. What is a parasite?*

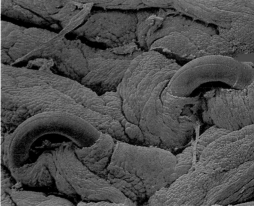

Figure 1–22 Trichinella *worms, which cause the disease trichinosis, burrow into the muscle tissue of their host (top). These threadworms, tunneling through the tissues of a sheep's small intestine, are parasitic roundworms (bottom).*

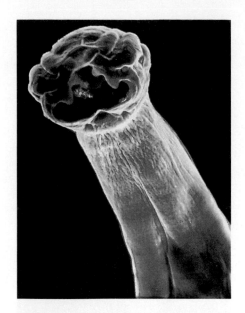

Figure 1–23 *Hookworms use the sharp teeth and hooks on their head end to burrow through their host's skin.*

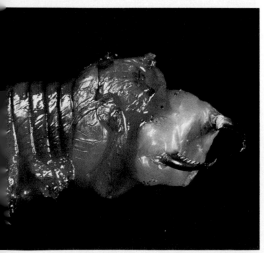

Figure 1–24 *Many segmented worms, such as the sandworm, use hooklike jaws to capture their prey. To which phylum of invertebrates do sandworms belong?*

Like all worms, roundworms have a head and a tail. In fact, worms were the first organisms to evolve with distinct head and tail ends. Roundworms have a tubelike digestive system that has two openings—a mouth and an anus (AY-nuhs). Food enters the digestive system through the mouth (in the head end) and waste products leave the digestive system through the anus (in the tail end). Although the digestive system of roundworms may not seem complex, it is far more advanced than that of cnidarians. As you may recall, cnidarians have one opening for both the intake of food and the elimination of wastes.

Segmented Worms

Segmented worms belong to the phylum Annelida (an-uh-LIHD-uh). The term annelid comes from the Latin word for ringed. This is an appropriate name for these invertebrates because their most obvious feature is a ringed, or segmented, body. These segments are visible on the outside of an annelid's body. Segmented worms live in salty oceans, in freshwater lakes and streams, or in the soil.

The segmented worm you are probably most familiar with is the common earthworm. The body of an earthworm is divided into numerous segments—100 at least. If you have ever touched an earthworm, you know it has a slimy outer layer. This layer, made of a slippery substance called mucus, helps the earthworm to glide through the soil. Tiny setae (SEE-tee; singular: seta), or bristles, on the segments of the earthworm also help it to pull itself along the ground.

As all gardeners know, earthworms are essential to a healthy garden. By burrowing through the soil, earthworms create tiny passageways through which air enters, thus improving the quality of the soil. As earthworms burrow, they feed on dead plant and animal matter. These materials are only partially digested. The undigested portions, or waste products, are eliminated into the surrounding soil, thus fertilizing the soil. The digestive system of an earthworm is shown in Figure 1–25.

Earthworms have a closed circulatory system. A closed circulatory system is one in which all body fluids are contained within small tubes. In an earthworm, the fluids are pumped throughout its body by a series of ringed blood vessels found near its head region. Because these blood vessels help to pump fluids through the circulatory system, they are sometimes called hearts.

Earthworms, like most annelids, have no special respiratory organs. Oxygen enters through the skin, and carbon dioxide leaves through the skin. In order for this to happen, the skin must stay moist. If an earthworm's skin dries out—which might happen if the earthworm remains out in the heat of the sun— the earthworm suffocates and dies.

Although earthworms have only a simple nervous system, they are very sensitive to their environment. An earthworm's nervous system consists of a brain found in the head region, two nerves that pass around the intestine, and a nerve cord located on the lower side.

In addition to these structures, an earthworm has a variety of cells that sense changes in its environment. One group of such cells, located on the first few body segments, detects moisture. Recall how important moisture is to an earthworm's survival. If an earthworm emerges from its burrow and encounters a dry spot, it will move from side to side until it finds dampness. If it does not find any moisture, it will retreat into its burrow. An earthworm can also sense danger and warn other earthworms. It does so by releasing a sweatlike material that helps it to glide more easily and to warn others of the nearby danger.

Worms at Work

1. Put a tall, thin can with the closed end up in a large jar. Fill the large jar with soil to the level of the tin can. Add a thin layer of sand.

2. Put five earthworms in the jar. Add pond water or tap water that has been standing for a day to slightly moisten the soil. Add more water if the soil appears dry.

3. Cover the outside of the jar with black paper and leave the jar undisturbed for a day.

4. Uncover the jar and look for the earthworms. Record your observations.

5. Cover the jar for one more day. Repeat step 4.

■ Have the earthworms been at work? Explain.

Figure 1–25 *The drawing shows the digestive system of the earthworm, a segmented worm. The photograph is of an earthworm moving along the surface of the soil. What structures help the earthworm move?*

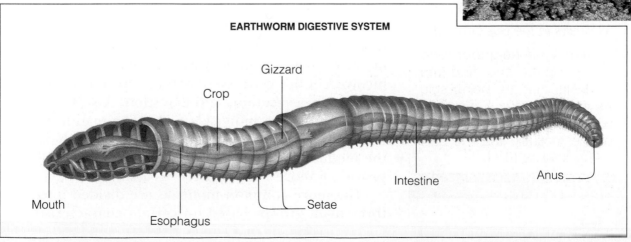

EARTHWORM DIGESTIVE SYSTEM

Crop

Gizzard

Mouth

Esophagus

Setae

Intestine

Anus

Figure 1–26 *An earthworm contains both male and female structures. When two earthworms mate, they exchange only sperm cells.*

1–5 Section Review

1. List the three phyla of worms and give an example of each.
2. Name two types of worms that cause disease in humans.
3. How does an earthworm contribute to a healthy garden?
4. In what ways are worms more complex than cnidarians?

Connection—*Medicine*

5. Imagine that you are a doctor. Recently a number of your patients have developed hookworm infections. Describe some actions you would prescribe to prevent others from being infected by hookworms.

Guide for Reading

Focus on these questions as you read.

▶ *What are the main characteristics of mollusks?*

▶ *What are the three main groups of mollusks?*

Aᴄᴛɪᴠɪᴛʏ

DOING

Mollusks in the Supermarket

Visit your neighborhood supermarket and find the mollusks that are being sold as food. Make a chart in which you include the name of the mollusk and the part being sold as food.

1–6 Mollusks

If you enjoy eating a variety of seafood, you are probably already familiar with some members of the phylum Mollusca (muh-ʟᴜʜs-kuh). Members of this phylum are called mollusks (ᴍᴀʜʟ-uhsks). Mollusks include clams, oysters, mussels, octopuses, and squids. The word mollusk comes from the Latin word meaning soft. **Mollusks are soft-bodied animals that typically have inner or outer shells.**

Most mollusks also have a thick muscular foot. Some mollusks use this foot to open and close their shell. Other mollusks use it for movement. Still others use the foot to bury themselves in the sand or mud.

The head region of a mollusk generally contains a mouth and sense organs such as eyes. The rest of a mollusk's body contains various organs that are involved in life processes such as reproduction, circulation, excretion, and digestion. A soft mantle covers much of a mollusk's body. The mantle produces the material that makes up the hard shell. As the mollusk grows, the mantle enlarges the shell, providing more room for its occupant.

The more common mollusks are divided into three main groups based on certain characteristics.

These characteristics include the presence of a shell, the type of shell, and the type of foot. **The three main groups of common mollusks are snails, slugs, and their relatives; two-shelled mollusks; and tentacled mollusks.**

Snails, Slugs, and Their Relatives

The largest group of common mollusks are those that have a single shell or no shell at all. The members of this group include snails, slugs, and sea butterflies, to name a few. These mollusks are also known as gastropods (GAS-troh-pahdz). The word gastropod means stomach foot. This name is appropriate because most gastropods move by means of a foot found on the same side of the body as their stomach. Gastropods live in both fresh water and salt water, as well as on land. Those gastropods that live on land, however, still must have a moist environment in order to survive.

Gastropods have an interesting feature called a radula (RAJ-oo-luh) in their mouth. The tongue-shaped radula resembles a file used by carpenters to scrape wood. The radula files off bits of plant matter into small pieces that can easily be swallowed.

The single-shelled gastropod that is probably most familiar to you is a garden snail. Have you ever watched a garden snail as it moves? If so, you might have noticed that it leaves a trail of slippery mucus behind. The mucus enables a snail to slowly glide across different types of surfaces. This is especially helpful when a snail encounters rough surfaces.

Slugs are gastropods that do not have a shell. The absence of a shell may seem to make slugs easy prey for their predators. But slugs are not entirely helpless. Most spend the daylight hours hiding under rocks and logs, thereby staying out of the way of birds and other animals that might eat them. Gastropods such as sea butterflies escape predators by rapidly swimming away. Many sea slugs, or nudibranchs (NOO-dih-brangks), have chemicals in their body that taste bad or are poisonous to unsuspecting predators.

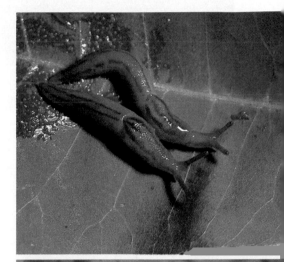

Figure 1–27 *Mollusks—such as garden slugs (top), coquina clams (center), and cuttlefish (bottom)—have soft bodies. Unlike most mollusks, which have internal or external shells, slugs lack shells completely.*

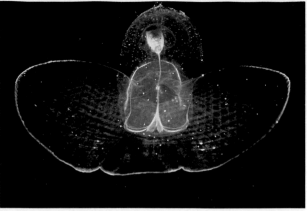

Figure 1–28 *Gastropods, the largest group of common mollusks, have a single shell or no shell at all. The single-shelled gastropod that is probably the most familiar to you is the land snail (left); whereas the sea butterfly (right) is not as common a sight. What are some other examples of gastropods?*

Activity Bank

Moving at a Snail's Pace, p.154

Figure 1–29 *Scallops can move around by clapping their shells together (left). A scallop is also able to gather information about its surroundings with the help of its eyes, which are located on the mantle and resemble tiny blue dots (right).*

Two-Shelled Mollusks

Clams, oysters, scallops, and mussels are members of the group of common mollusks called bivalves, or two-shelled mollusks. Bivalves have two shells that are held together by powerful muscles. Although most bivalves remain in one place, scallops and a few others can move around rapidly by clapping their shells together. This action forces water out between the shells, thereby propelling the bivalve.

Unlike gastropods, bivalves do not have a radula. Instead, they are filter feeders. This means that as water passes over the body of a bivalve, the bivalve filters out small organisms.

The mantle of a bivalve, like that of most mollusks, contains glands that produce its shell. These glands keep the inside surfaces of the shell smooth. If a foreign object, such as a grain of sand, gets stuck between the mantle and the shell of some types of mollusks, the glands cover it with a shiny secretion. After a few years, the grain of sand becomes completely covered with secretions and is called a pearl.

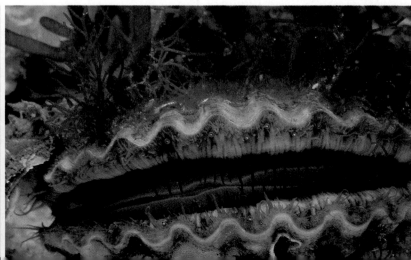

Tentacled Mollusks

The most highly developed mollusks are the tentacled mollusks. The tentacled mollusks are also called cephalopods (SEHF-uh-loh-pahdz). Included in this group are octopuses, squids, and nautiluses. Most cephalopods do not have an outer shell but have some part of a shell within their body. The one exception is the chambered nautilus. The chambered nautilus got its name from the fact that its shell consists of many chambers. These chambers are small when the animal is young but increase in size as the animal grows. As the nautilus grows, it builds a new outer chamber in which it lives.

All cephalopods have tentacles that they use to move themselves and to capture food. But the number and type of tentacles differ from one kind of cephalopod to another. Octopuses, of course, have eight tentacles (the prefix *octo-* means eight); squids have ten.

Even though most cephalopods do not have an outer shell, they do have ways to protect themselves. Most cephalopods can move quickly by either swimming or crawling. Octopuses, squids, and nautiluses can also move by using a form of jet propulsion. Water is drawn into the mantle cavity and then forced out through a tube, propelling the cephalopod backward—away from the danger. In addition, squids and octopuses produce a dark-colored ink when they are frightened. As this ink is released into the water, it helps to hide the mollusk and confuse its predators. The squid or octopus can then escape.

Figure 1–30 *The nautilus (top), squid (center), and octopus (bottom) are examples of cephalopods. What are some characteristics of cephalopods?*

1–6 Section Review

1. What are the main characteristics of mollusks?
2. How are mollusks grouped?
3. List the three main groups of mollusks and give an example of each.
4. What is a mantle? A radula?

Critical Thinking—*Relating Facts*
5. Suppose you found a mollusk with one shell and eyes located on two stalks sticking out of its head. Into which group of mollusks would you place it? Explain.

Laboratory Investigation

Observing Earthworm Responses

Problem

How do earthworms respond to changes in their environment?

Materials (per group)

2 live earthworms in a storage container
medicine dropper
paper towels
tray
piece of cardboard
desk lamp

Procedure 🔬 ⚗️ 🛏️

1. Open the storage container and examine the earthworms. Record your observations of their physical characteristics. Fill the medicine dropper with water and use it to give your earthworms a "bath." **Note:** *Make sure you keep your earthworms moist by giving them frequent baths.*

2. Fold a dry paper towel and place it on one side of your tray. Fold a moistened paper towel and place it on the other side of the tray.

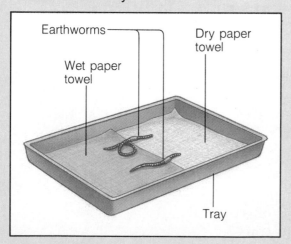

Earthworms
Dry paper towel
Wet paper towel
Tray

3. Place the earthworms in the center of the tray, between the dry paper towel and the moist paper towel. Cover the tray with the piece of cardboard.

4. After 5 minutes, remove the cardboard and observe the location of the earthworms. Record your observations.

5. Return the earthworms to their storage container. Using the dropper, moisten the earthworms with water.

6. Cover the entire bottom of the tray with a moistened paper towel.

7. Place the earthworms in the center of the tray.

8. Cover one half of the tray with the piece of cardboard. Position the lamp above the uncovered side of the tray.

9. After 5 minutes, observe the location of the earthworms. Record your observations.

10. Return the earthworms to their storage container. Using the dropper, moisten the earthworms with water. Cover the container and return it to your teacher.

Observations

Describe the earthworms' color, texture, external features, and other physical characteristics.

Analysis and Conclusions

1. How does an earthworm's response to moisture help it to survive?

2. Does an earthworm's response to light have any protective value? Explain.

3. How is an earthworm's body adapted for movement through the soil?

4. Would you expect to find earthworms in hard soil? Explain.

Summarizing Key Concepts

1–1 The Five Kingdoms

▲ Today, the most generally accepted classification system contains five kingdoms: monerans, protists, fungi, plants, and animals.

1–2 Introduction to the Animal Kingdom

▲ Vertebrates are animals with a backbone. Invertebrates are animals without a backbone.

1–3 Sponges

▲ Sponges belong to the phylum Porifera. They are called poriferans because their bodies are covered with many pores.

▲ The cells of sponges remove food and oxygen from ocean water as the water flows through pores. The water flowing out through a larger opening carries away waste products.

▲ Sexual reproduction is the process by which a new organism forms from the joining of a female cell (egg) and a male cell (sperm).

▲ Asexual reproduction is the process by which a single organism produces a new organism.

1–4 Cnidarians

▲ Cnidarians belong to the phylum Cnidaria. They have a hollow central cavity with one opening called the mouth.

▲ Cnidarians have structures called nematocysts on the tentacles around their mouth.

1–5 Worms

▲ The three main groups of worms are flatworms, roundworms, and segmented worms.

▲ Flatworms, members of the phylum Platyhelminthes, have flat bodies and live in ponds and streams.

▲ Organisms that grow on or in other living things are called parasites. The organism upon which a parasite lives is called the host.

▲ Roundworms are members of the phylum Nematoda.

▲ Segmented worms, or annelids, have segmented bodies and live in soil or in salt water or fresh water.

1–6 Mollusks

▲ Mollusks, members of the phylum Mollusca, are animals with soft bodies that typically have inner or outer shells.

▲ Most mollusks have a thick, muscular foot and are covered by a mantle.

Reviewing Key Terms

Define each term in a complete sentence.

1–1 The Five Kingdoms
kingdom
autotroph
heterotroph

1–2 Introduction to the Animal Kingdom
vertebrate
invertebrate

1–3 Sponges
spicule
sexual reproduction
asexual reproduction

1–4 Cnidarians
nematocyst

1–5 Worms
regeneration
parasite
host

Chapter Review

Content Review

Multiple Choice

Choose the letter of the answer that best completes each statement.

1. The largest and most general group in the classification system is the
   a. phylum.
   b. kingdom.
   c. species.
   d. class.

2. Organisms that can make their own food are called
   a. protists.
   b. heterotrophs.
   c. fungi.
   d. autotrophs.

3. Which is an invertebrate?
   a. lion
   b. human
   c. dog
   d. jellyfish

4. Which animal is a member of the phylum Porifera?
   a. sponge
   b. coral
   c. planarian
   d. squid

5. Cnidarians have
   a. pores.
   b. a mouth and an anus.
   c. mantles.
   d. nematocysts.

6. Which animal is a flatworm?
   a. hydra
   b. sea anemone
   c. planarian
   d. jellyfish

7. The animal that causes trichinosis is a
   a. roundworm.
   b. flatworm.
   c. segmented worm.
   d. cnidarian.

8. Tapeworms are
   a. sponges.
   b. flatworms.
   c. cnidarians.
   d. mollusks.

9. All mollusks have
   a. outer shells.
   b. soft bodies.
   c. nematocysts.
   d. spicules.

10. Clams are
    a. cnidarians.
    b. mollusks.
    c. flatworms.
    d. roundworms.

True or False

If the statement is true, write "true." If it is false, change the underlined word or words to make the statement true.

1. Animals are multicellular <u>autotrophs</u>.
2. <u>Invertebrates</u> have no backbone.
3. All <u>sponges</u> have <u>pores</u>.
4. Nematocysts are found in <u>mollusks</u>.
5. <u>Flatworms</u> are nematodes.
6. In <u>segmented worms</u>, the mantle produces the shell.
7. An oyster is an example of a <u>tentacled mollusk</u>.
8. The octopus is a <u>cnidarian</u>.

Concept Mapping

Complete the following concept map for Section 1–1. Refer to pages C6–C7 to construct a concept map for the entire chapter.

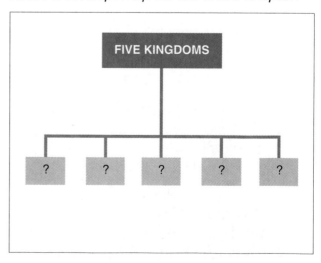

Concept Mastery

Discuss each of the following in a brief paragraph.

1. Why do you think it is important to study animals?
2. List the five kingdoms of living things and give a description of each.
3. Describe the similarities and differences among the three groups of mollusks.
4. List the different methods sponges, cnidarians, worms, and mollusks use to get food.
5. Describe how sponges take in oxygen and give off carbon dioxide.
6. In what ways are sponges useful?
7. Compare a medusa and a polyp.
8. Why are tapeworms parasites?
9. How are mollusks useful?
10. Compare sexual reproduction and asexual reproduction.

Critical Thinking and Problem Solving

Use the skills you have developed in this chapter to answer each of the following.

1. **Making charts** Construct a chart in which you list each phylum of invertebrates discussed in this chapter, the major characteristics of the phylum, and two examples from each phylum.
2. **Applying concepts** Why is it that scientists do not classify animals by what they eat or where they live?
3. **Making generalizations** In what ways are earthworms beneficial to humans?
4. **Designing an experiment** The eyes of a squid are similar in structure to the eyes of a vertebrate. Design an experiment to determine whether or not squids are able to see color. Include a hypothesis, control, and variable.
5. **Relating cause and effect** People with tapeworms eat a lot but still feel hungry and tired. Why?
6. **Making predictions** Would it be safe to eat clams from polluted water? Give a logical reason for your answer.
7. **Relating facts** Explain this statement: In a classification system, an organism is identified by showing what it is not.
8. **Using the writing process** Imagine that you could shrink down to a size small enough to fit inside an earthworm. Describe the adventures you and the earthworm would have in a garden one summer day.

Arthropods and Echinoderms

Guide for Reading

After you read the following sections, you will be able to

2–1 Arthropods: The "Joint-Footed" Animals

- Describe the characteristics of arthropods.
- Identify the major groups of arthropods.

2–2 Insects: The Most Numerous Arthropods

- Describe the characteristics of insects.
- Explain how insects behave.

2–3 Echinoderms: The "Spiny-Skinned" Animals

- Describe the characteristics of echinoderms.

As darkness falls on a warm summer evening, fireflies light their "lanterns." The temperature has to be warm enough and the late-day light dim enough for them to be seen. If these conditions prevail, the tiny magicians light up the night worldwide.

A firefly's light is one of nature's marvels. It is light with almost no heat—a feat humans have yet to achieve. In fact, a firefly's light is cooler than the warm night air that surrounds it.

The greatest firefly show in the world occurs during summer evenings in Thailand. Male fireflies bunch together on certain trees that line the rivers. Flashing 120 times a minute, the male fireflies soon regulate their flashes so that at one instant there is total blackness, and at the next instant total illumination—over and over again!

Fireflies (which are actually beetles, not flies) belong to a phylum of invertebrates called arthropods. In this chapter you will read about this phylum of fascinating creatures. And you will also be introduced to another phylum of invertebrates, the echinoderms, which includes the lovely yet somewhat dangerous purple sea urchin.

Journal *Activity*

You and Your World Think of a place near your home or school where animals may live. It can be a schoolyard, a backyard, an empty lot, a park, or even an alley. It should have some soil, rocks, green plants, and a source of moisture. Write a detailed description of the area in your journal. Draw a picture of it. Then visit the area and see if your description was accurate. Make any necessary changes in your journal.

◄ *The Thailand night is illuminated by an awesome firefly show.*

Guide for Reading

Focus on these questions as you read.

▶ What are the main characteristics of arthropods?

▶ What are the characteristics of each of the four groups of arthropods?

2–1 Arthropods: The "Joint-Footed" Animals

The phylum of invertebrates that contains the greatest number of species is the phylum Arthropoda (ahr-THRAHP-uh-duh). Members of this phylum are called arthropods. To date, more than 1 million species of arthropods have been described. Scientists estimate, however, that the total number of arthropod species may be as high as 1 billion billion, or 1,000,000,000,000,000,000! Arthropods live in air, on land, and in water. Wherever you happen to live, you can be sure arthropods live there too. Arthropods are our main competitors for food. In fact, if left alone and unchecked, they could eventually take over the Earth!

Why are there so many arthropods? One reason is that they have been evolving (changing) on Earth for more than 600 million years. During this time, they have developed certain characteristics that allowed them to become so successful. Of these characteristics, three are common to all arthropods. **The three characteristics shared by all arthropods are an exoskeleton, a segmented body, and jointed appendages.**

Figure 2–1 *The spider crab (top left), millipede (top right), daddy longlegs (bottom right), and weevil and ant (bottom left) are members of the largest and most diverse group of invertebrates: the arthropods. What three characteristics are shared by all arthropods?*

The most striking characteristic of arthropods is the **exoskeleton.** An exoskeleton is a rigid outer covering. The exoskeletons of many land-dwelling arthropods are waterproof. Such exoskeletons limit the loss of water from the bodies of arthropods, thus making it possible for them to live in remarkably dry environments such as deserts. In some ways, an exoskeleton is like the armor worn by knights in the Middle Ages as protection in battle. One drawback of an exoskeleton, however, is that it does not grow as the animal grows. So the arthropod's protective suit must be shed and replaced from time to time. This process is called **molting.** While the exoskeleton is replacing itself, the arthropod is more vulnerable to attack from other animals.

Like annelids (segmented worms), arthropods have segmented bodies. This characteristic strongly suggests that annelids and arthropods evolved from a common ancestor. The body of most arthropods, however, is shorter and has fewer segments than an annelid's.

Although the phylum name, Arthropoda, comes from the Greek words meaning jointed legs, it is not just legs that enable arthropods to move. The appendages characteristic of arthropods include antennae, claws, walking legs, and wings as well. See Figure 2–4 on page 42.

An arthropod has an open circulatory system, or one in which the blood is not contained within small tubes. Instead, the blood is pumped by a heart throughout the spaces within the arthropod's body.

Figure 2–2 *In order to increase in size, arthropods must molt, or shed their exoskeletons. This adult cicada is emerging from its exoskeleton, which it has outgrown.*

Figure 2–3 *Some arthropods, such as the Hawaiian lobster and dust mite have hard, tough exoskeletons. Other arthropods, such as the Promethea moth caterpillar, have flexible exoskeletons. What is an exoskeleton?*

Figure 2-4 *Arthropod appendages include the antennae of a harlequin beetle, the claws of a fiddler crab, the legs of a praying mantis, and the wings of a green lacewing fly.*

Activity Bank

Off and Running, p.156

ACTIVITY READING

A Silky Story

You may want to read a wonderful story about an exceptional spider named Charlotte who weaves messages into her web. The book is entitled *Charlotte's Web,* and it was written by E. B. White.

Although an arthropod's blood carries food throughout its body, it does not carry oxygen. Oxygen is carried to all the cells by one (sometimes two) of three basic respiratory (breathing) organs—gills, book lungs, and a system of air tubes.

Arthropods reproduce sexually. That means there are two parents, a male and a female. The male produces sperm, and the female produces eggs. In most arthropods, the sperm and the egg unite inside the body of the female.

Various animals make up this phylum. They include crustaceans (kruhs-TAY-shuhnz), centipedes and millipedes, spiders and their relatives, and insects.

Crustaceans

Do you see the two eyes peering out at you from the shell in Figure 2–5? These eyes belong to an animal known as a hermit crab. A hermit crab is a crustacean that lives in shells discarded by other water-dwelling animals such as mollusks. A crustacean is an arthropod that has a hard exoskeleton, two pairs of antennae, and mouthparts that are used for crushing and grinding food. Crustaceans include crabs, lobsters, barnacles, and shrimp.

The body of a crustacean is divided into segments. A pair of appendages is attached to each segment. The type of appendage varies, depending on the crustacean. Crabs, for example, have claws. The claws of some crabs are so strong that they can be used to open a crab's favorite food, a coconut. Crabs also have walking legs and antennae, which are some other examples of appendages.

Crustaceans such as crabs are able to regenerate (regrow) certain parts of their body. The stone crab, which lives in the waters off the coast of Florida, can grow new claws. This is an important characteristic for a stone crab because its claws are considered particularly tasty by people. When a stone crab is caught, one of its claws is broken off and the stone crab is returned to the water. In about a year's time, the missing claw is regenerated. If a crab is caught again, that claw may once again be removed.

Most crustaceans live in watery environments and obtain oxygen from the water through special respiratory organs called gills. Even the few land-dwelling crustaceans have gills. Such crustaceans, however, must live in damp areas in order to get oxygen.

Figure 2–5 *Water-dwelling crustaceans include the hermit crab and goose neck barnacles.*

Figure 2–6 *The diagram shows some of the internal and external structures of a crayfish.*

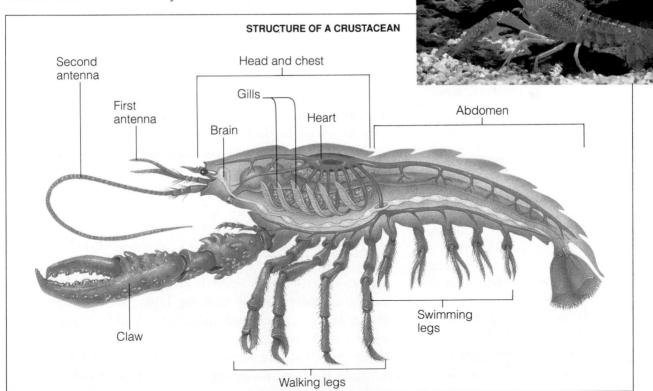

STRUCTURE OF A CRUSTACEAN

Second antenna

First antenna

Head and chest

Gills

Brain

Heart

Abdomen

Claw

Swimming legs

Walking legs

Figure 2–7 *Although a centipede (top) and a millipede (bottom) look very much alike, they do differ in some ways. What are two ways in which centipedes and millipedes differ?*

Centipedes and Millipedes

Centipedes and millipedes are arthropods that have many legs. What distinguishes one from the other is that centipedes have one pair of legs in each segment, whereas millipedes have two pairs of legs in each segment.

If you were an earthworm crawling through the soil, you would certainly be aware of another difference between centipedes and millipedes. Millipedes live on plants and thus would simply pass you by. Millipedes are shy creatures. When disturbed, millipedes may roll up into a ball to protect themselves. Centipedes, on the other hand, are carnivores, or flesh eaters. They are active hunters. To capture you, a centipede would inject poison into your body through its claws. (Another difference between centipedes and millipedes is that centipedes have claws and millipedes do not.)

Unlike many arthropods, the exoskeletons of centipedes and millipedes are not waterproof. To avoid excessive water loss, centipedes and millipedes are usually found in damp places such as under rocks or in soil.

Spiders and Their Relatives

There is a legend in Greek mythology about a young woman named Arachne (uh-RAK-nee) who challenged the goddess Athena to a weaving contest. When Arachne won the contest, Athena tore up Arachne's tapestry. Arachne hanged herself in sorrow. Athena then changed Arachne into a spider and Arachne's tapestry into a spider's web. Today spiders, as well as scorpions, ticks, and mites, are included in a group of arthropods called arachnids (uh-RAK-nihdz). As you can see, the word arachnid comes from the name Arachne.

The body of an arachnid is divided into two parts: a head and chest part and an abdomen part. Although arachnids vary in size and shape, they all have four pairs (8) of walking legs. So if you ever find a small animal you think is a spider, count its legs to make sure.

Spiders usually feed on insects. A few types of tropical spiders, however, can catch and eat small

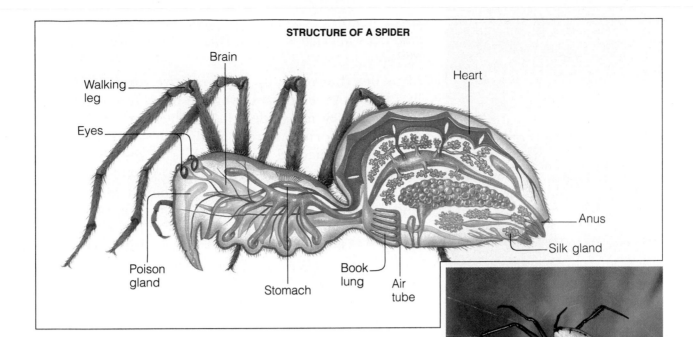

STRUCTURE OF A SPIDER

Brain

Walking leg

Heart

Eyes

Anus

Silk gland

Poison gland

Stomach

Book lung

Air tube

vertebrates such as hummingbirds. Spiders catch their prey in different ways. Many make webs of fine, yet very strong, flexible material called silk. Silk is secreted by special structures located in a spider's abdomen. Many spiders weave a new web every day. At night, the spiders eat the strands of that day's web, recycling the material the following day when they produce a new web. Although many spiders do not spin webs, they all produce silk. The silk that makes up the web is five times stronger than steel!

Some spiders hide from their prey and then suddenly jump out, taking the unsuspecting victim by surprise. For example, the trapdoor spider lives in a hole in the ground covered by a door made of silk. The door itself is hidden by soil and bits of plants. When an unsuspecting insect passes close to the trapdoor, the trapdoor spider jumps out and catches the unlucky victim.

Once a spider catches its prey, it injects venom, or poison, into the prey through a pair of fangs. Sometimes the venom kills the prey immediately. Other times it only paralyzes the prey. In this way, the spider can preserve living creatures trapped in its web for a time when it needs more food.

Most spiders get their oxygen by means of respiratory organs called book lungs. This is an appropriate name for these organs because the several sheets

Figure 2–8 *Spiders such as the orchard spider (top) and flower crab spider (bottom) belong to the group of arthropods called arachnids. Compare the structures that you see in the photographs with those shown in the diagram of the spider. How many legs do arachnids have?*

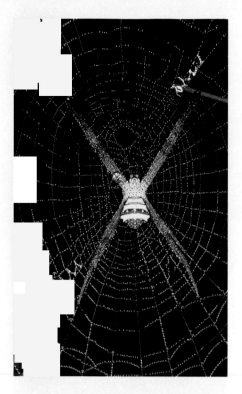

Figure 2-9 *Some spiders, such as the orb weaver spider, build webs to catch their prey. What material makes up the web?*

of tissues that make up the structure resemble pages in a book. As air passes over the book lungs, oxygen is removed. Some spiders, however, have respiratory organs that form a system of air tubes. These air tubes are connected to the outside of the spider's body through small openings in its exoskeleton.

Arachnids live in many environments. Most spiders live on land. One interesting exception is a spider that lives under water inside bubbles of air that it carries down from the surface. When the air bubbles are used up, the spider returns to the water's surface for a fresh supply.

Scorpions are generally found in dry desert areas. Scorpions are active primarily at night. During the day, they hide under logs, stones, or in holes in the ground. People who enjoy camping must be careful

Figure 2-10 *Spiders capture their prey in several ways. The trapdoor spider (left) lies in wait and then leaps out to grab unlucky insects. The wolf spider (bottom right) hides in burrows in the sand waiting for its unsuspecting prey. The tarantula (top right) is large enough to catch and eat small invertebrates.*

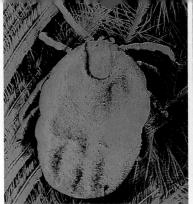

when they put on their shoes or boots in the morning: A scorpion may have mistaken the footwear for a suitable place in which to escape from the heat of the day! When scorpions capture prey, they hold it with their large front claws and, at the same time, inject it with venom through the stingers in their tails.

Ticks and mites live on other organisms. They may live on a plant and stay in one place, or they may live on an animal and travel wherever the animal travels. Like certain flatworms and roundworms, ticks and mites live off the body fluids of plants and animals. Some live by sucking juices from the stems and leaves of plants. Other ticks and mites are very tiny and live on insects. Many ticks suck blood from larger animals. In the process, they may spread disease. For example, Rocky Mountain spotted fever and Lyme disease are spread to people through the bites of ticks.

2–1 Section Review

1. What are the three main characteristics of arthropods?
2. What is an exoskeleton?
3. List four groups of arthropods.
4. What are some ways in which spiders and their relatives catch prey?

Critical Thinking—*Applying Concepts*
5. Blue crabs usually have hard shells. During certain times of the year, however, some blue crabs have thin, papery shells and are called soft-shell crabs. In terms of the life processes of arthropods, explain why these blue crabs have soft shells.

Figure 2–11 *Notice the stinger at the end of the scorpion's tail. The wood tick and the red velvet mites, which are devouring a termite, are arachnids.*

Activity Bank

Spinning Webs, p.157

ACTIVITY

DISCOVERING

The Life of a Mealworm

1. Fill a clean 1-liter jar about one third full of bran cereal.

2. Place four mealworms in the jar.

3. Add a few slices of raw potato to the jar.

4. Shred a newspaper and place it loosely in the jar.

5. Cover the top of the jar with a layer of cheesecloth. Use a rubber band to hold the cheesecloth in place.

6. Observe the jar at least once a week for 4 weeks. Record all changes that take place in the mealworms.

How long was the mealworms' life cycle?

■ Do mealworms undergo complete or incomplete metamorphosis? Explain.

2–2 Insects: The Most Numerous Arthropods

Perhaps you have noticed that one group of arthropods mentioned in the previous section has not yet been discussed. This group, of course, is the insects. It would be hard to overlook insects for long. After all, there are more kinds of insects than there are all other animal species combined. In fact, it has been estimated that there may be as many as 300 million insects for every person on Earth!

Insect Structure

Insects are described as having a body that is divided into three parts—a head, a chest, and an abdomen—and that has three pairs (6) of legs attached to the chest part. In a grasshopper, which is a typical insect, the three pairs of legs are not identical. In order for a grasshopper to jump, one pair of legs must be larger than the other two pairs. Which pair of legs do you think is larger: the front pair or the back pair?

If you look closely at the head of a grasshopper, you will see five eyes peering back at you. Three of these eyes are located on the front of the grasshopper's head and are called simple eyes. Simple eyes can detect only light and dark. The remaining two

Figure 2-12 *Compare this grasshopper with the diagram of the structure of a grasshopper. How many legs does an insect have?*

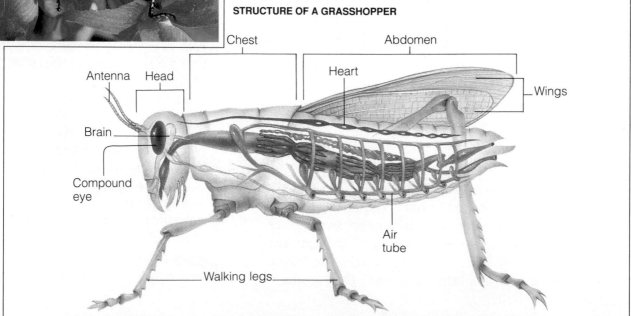

STRUCTURE OF A GRASSHOPPER

Chest

Abdomen

Heart

Antenna   Head

Wings

Brain

Compound eye

Air tube

Walking legs

eyes, which are found on each side of the grasshopper's head, are called compound eyes. Compound eyes contain many lenses. Although compound eyes can distinguish some colors, they are best at detecting movement. This ability is important to an animal that is hunted by other animals on a daily basis.

Like most insects, a grasshopper has wings—two pairs of wings, in fact. Although these wings are best suited for short distances, some types of grasshoppers can fly great distances in search of food. Insect flight varies from the gentle fluttering motion of a butterfly to the speedy movement of a hawkmoth, which can fly as fast as 50 kilometers per hour!

Like all insects, a grasshopper does not have a well-developed system for getting oxygen into its body and removing waste gases from its body. What a grasshopper does have is a system of tubes that carries oxygen through the exoskeleton and into its body.

Male grasshoppers produce sperm, and female grasshoppers produce eggs. Like most insects, a male grasshopper deposits sperm inside a female grasshopper during reproduction.

Growth and Development of Insects

Insects spend a great deal of time eating. As a result, they grow rapidly. And like other arthropods, insects must shed their exoskeletons as they grow. During the growth process, insects pass through several stages of development. Some species of insects change their appearance completely as they pass through the different stages. This dramatic change in form is known as **metamorphosis** (meht-uh-MOR-fuh-sihs). The word metamorphosis comes from the Greek words meaning to transform. There are two types of metamorphosis: complete and incomplete.

During complete metamorphosis, insects such as butterflies, beetles, bees, and moths pass through a four-stage process. The first stage produces an egg. When an egg hatches, a **larva** (LAHR-vuh) emerges, completing the second stage. A caterpillar is the larva of an insect that will one day become a butterfly or a moth. Maggots are the larvae of flies, and grubs are the larvae of some types of beetles. A larva spends almost all its time eating.

Figure 2–13 *Insects such as the horsefly have compound eyes. Within the eyes are many lenses that enable the insect to detect the slightest movement of an object.*

Figure 2–14 *Insects, birds, and bats are the only organisms that can fly on their own. Like all insects, the painted beauty butterfly and the drone fly have two pairs of wings.*

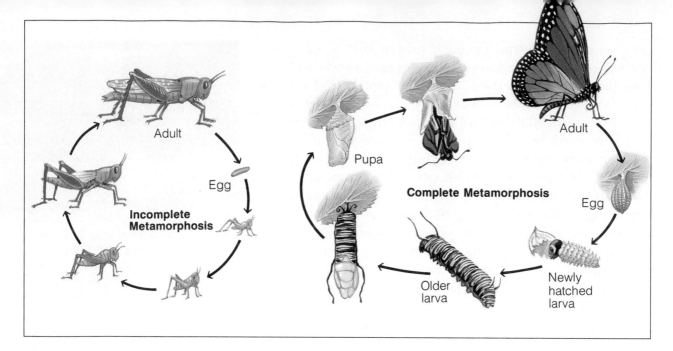

Adult

Egg

Incomplete Metamorphosis

Pupa

Complete Metamorphosis

Adult

Egg

Older larva

Newly hatched larva

Figure 2–15 *The monarch butterfly (right) undergoes complete metamorphosis, whereas the grasshopper (left) undergoes incomplete metamorphosis. What is another name for the older larva of a monarch butterfly?*

Figure 2–16 *The monarch butterfly begins life as an egg and then becomes a larva, also known as a caterpillar. During the pupa stage, the caterpillar wraps itself into a cocoon called a chrysalis. Finally, the butterfly emerges.*

Eventually, a larva enters the third stage, which produces a **pupa** (PYOO-puh; plural: pupae). Pupae are sometimes wrapped in a covering called a cocoon or chrysalis (KRIHS-uh-lihs). A cocoon is made of silk or other similar material. During this stage, remarkable changes take place, and an adult insect soon emerges. The adult signals the last stage of complete metamorphosis. An adult insect not only looks like a different animal, it also behaves differently.

During incomplete metamorphosis—which occurs in insects such as grasshoppers, termites, and dragonflies—young animals looking very much like the adults hatch from eggs. See Figure 2–15. These young animals do not have the organs of an adult, however, and they often do not have wings either. As the young animals grow, they keep molting (shedding

their exoskeletons) and getting larger until they reach adult size. Along the way, the young animals acquire all the characteristics of an adult animal.

Insect Behavior

Most insects live solitary lives. In this way, they do not compete directly with other members of their species for available food. Male and female insects, however, do interact in order to reproduce. But before they do, they must attract or signal each other. This is done in a variety of ways, depending on the insects. For example, to attract a female, the male cicada (sih-KAY-duh) buzzes by, vibrating a special membrane in its abdomen. A male firefly attracts a female firefly, which in some species is called a glowworm, by turning the light-producing organ in its abdomen on and off. The female gypsy moth attracts a male by releasing extremely powerful chemicals called **pheromones** (FER-uh-mohnz). Pheromones cannot be detected by humans, but only a small amount of pheromones can attract a male gypsy moth from several kilometers downwind.

Other insects, known as social insects, cannot survive alone. These insects form colonies, or hives. Ants, termites, some wasp species, and bees are social insects. They survive as a society of individual insects that perform different jobs. As you can see in Figure 2–18, many of these colonies are highly organized.

One of the most fascinating examples of an insect society is a beehive. A beehive is a marvel of organization. Worker bees, which are all females, perform

Figure 2–17 *A male luna moth's feathery antennae can detect pheromones released by a female luna moth several kilometers away. What are pheromones?*

Figure 2–18 *It may be hard to believe, but this mound was built by termites (left)! Termites, carpenter ants (center), and honeybees (right) are examples of social insects. How do social insects differ from most other insects?*

How Many Are Too Many?, p.159

all the tasks necessary for the survival of the hive. Worker bees supply the other members of the hive with food by making honey and the combs in which the honey is stored. They also feed the queen bee, whose only function is to produce an enormous number of eggs. In addition, worker bees clean and protect the hive. Male bees have only one function: to fertilize a queen's eggs.

Defense Mechanisms of Insects

Insects have many defense mechanisms that enable them to survive. Wasps and bees use stingers to defend themselves against enemies. Other insects are masters of camouflage (KAM-uh-flahj). This means that they can hide from their enemies by blending into their surroundings. For example, insects such as the stick grasshoppers resemble sticks and twigs. These insects survive because their bodies are not easily seen by their predators. See Figure 2–19.

Figure 2–19 *Insects defend themselves in a variety of ways. The tropical walking stick (top right) blends in with its surroundings so that it can hide from its predators. The bombardier beetle (bottom right) sprays a foul-smelling chemical. The peacock moth (bottom left) has eyespots that startle predators. How do you think the thorn bug (top left) defends itself?*

PROBLEM Solving

Do You Want to Dance?

How do honeybees communicate information about the type, quality, direction, and distance of a food source to other members of the hive? The answer is that they do a little dance. Actually, they do two basic dances: a round dance and a waggle dance.

In the round dance, the honeybee scout that has found food circles first in one direction and then in the other up the honeycomb, over and over again. This dance tells the other honeybees that food is within 50 meters of the hive.

In the waggle dance, the honeybee scout that has found food runs straight up the honeycomb while waggling her abdomen, circles in one direction, runs straight again, and then circles in the other direction. This dance tells the other honeybees that food is more than 50 meters away from the hive. If food is located toward the sun, the honeybee scout will run straight up the honeycomb in the same direction as the sun. If food is located 30° to the right of the sun, she will make a series of runs to the right of an imaginary vertical line on the honeycomb. If food is located 30° to the left of the sun, the same dance will be performed to the left of the imaginary line.

Use the four diagrams to answer the questions that follow.

1. Where is food located in Diagram C?

2. How far away is food in Diagram B: less than 50 meters or more than 50 meters?

3. Where is food located in Diagram A?

4. How far away is food in Diagram D: less than 50 meters or more than 50 meters?

Applying Facts

■ If you were a honeybee scout, how would you tell your hivemates that food is located more than 50 meters from the hive and 40° to the left of the sun?

■ Do honeybee scouts do waggle dances at night? Explain.

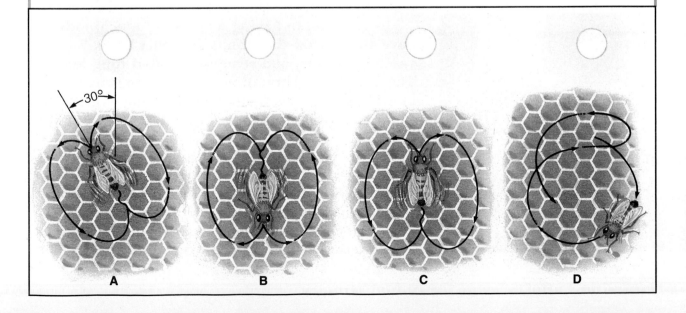

30°

A   B   C   D

1. What are the characteristics of insects?
2. What is metamorphosis? What are the four stages of metamorphosis in a butterfly?
3. How do social insects live?
4. How do insects defend themselves?

Connection—*Ecology*

5. Which method of insect control would be considered more environmentally safe: the use of pheromones or the use of chemicals known as pesticides? Explain.

Guide for Reading

Focus on this question as you read.

▶ *What are the characteristics of echinoderms?*

Figure 2–20 *Starfishes such as the ochre sea star use their tube feet to open mussels.*

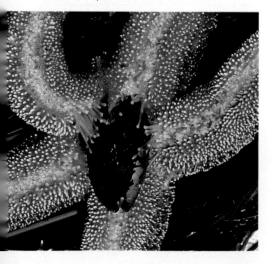

2–3 Echinoderms: The "Spiny-Skinned" Animals

Have you ever seen a starfish? Look at the photograph in Figure 2–21. It shows some interesting examples of invertebrates that belong to the phylum Echinodermata (ee-kihg-noh-DER-muh-tuh). Members of this phylum are called echinoderms. Echinoderms include starfishes, sea lilies, feather stars, sea cucumbers, sea urchins, and sand dollars—to name just a few. The word echinoderm comes from the Greek words meaning spiny skin. As their name indicates, members of this phylum are spiny-skinned animals.

In addition to having a spiny skin, echinoderms have an internal skeleton, a five-part body, a water vascular system, and structures called tube feet. The internal skeleton of an echinoderm is made of bonylike plates of calcium that are bumpy or spiny. The **water vascular system** is a system of fluid-filled internal tubes that carry food and oxygen, remove wastes, and help echinoderms move. These tubes open to the outside through a strainerlike structure. This structure connects to other tubes, which eventually connect to the suction-cuplike **tube feet**. All echinoderms use their tube feet to "walk." Some echinoderms also use them to get food.

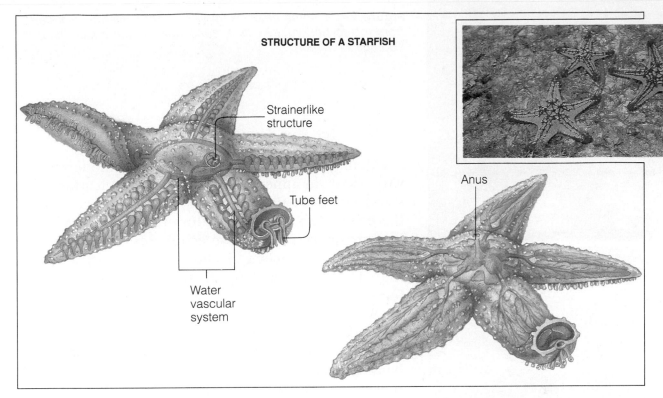

STRUCTURE OF A STARFISH

Strainerlike structure

Tube feet

Water vascular system

Anus

Starfishes

Although starfishes are not fish, most of them are shaped like stars. For this reason, starfishes are also called sea stars. Those that are star shaped have five or more arms, or rays, extending from a central body. On the underside of the arms are hundreds of tube feet that resemble tiny suction cups. These tube feet help the animal to move about and to obtain food. When a starfish passes over a clam, which is one of its favorite foods, the tiny tube feet grasp the clam's shell. The suction action of the hundreds of tube feet creates a tremendous force on the clam's shell. Eventually, the shell opens and the starfish enjoys a tasty meal.

People who harvest clams from the ocean bottom have long been at war with starfish that destroy the clam beds. In the past, starfishes captured near clam beds were cut into pieces and thrown back into the ocean. The people soon learned that, like flatworms and some crustaceans, starfishes have the ability to regenerate. By cutting them up, the people were guaranteeing that there would always be more and more starfishes—exactly the opposite of what they wanted to do.

Figure 2–21 *Echinoderm means spiny skin, which as you can see from this photograph of starfishes is an appropriate name for members of this phylum.*

Figure 2–22 *This sea star regenerated from a single arm.*

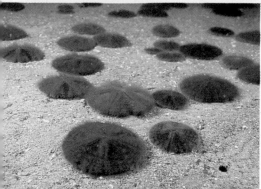

Figure 2–23 *Some other examples of echinoderms include, from top to bottom, sea lilies, sand dollars, sea cucumbers, and sea urchins.*

Other Echinoderms

Members of the other groups of echinoderms vary widely in appearance. Sea lilies and feather stars, which are thought to be the most ancient of the echinoderms, look like flowers and stars with long, feathery arms. These echinoderms spend most of their time attached or clinging to the ocean bottom. They use their long, feathery arms to gather food from the surrounding water.

Sea cucumbers, as their name implies, resemble warty cucumbers, with a mouth at one end and an anus at the other. These animals are usually found lying on the bottom of the ocean. Sea cucumbers move along the ocean bottom by using the five rows of tube feet on their body surface to wiggle back and forth.

Sea urchins and sand dollars are round shaped and rayless. Sand dollars are flat, whereas sea urchins are dome shaped. Many sea urchins have long spines that they use for protection. In some of these sea urchins, poisonous sacs found at the tip of each spine can deliver painful stings.

2–3 Section Review

1. What are the characteristics of echinoderms?
2. List some examples of echinoderms.
3. What are two functions of a starfish's tube feet?
4. Why is cutting up a starfish and throwing it back into the ocean an ineffective way of reducing a population of starfishes?

Critical Thinking—*Making Comparisons*
5. What are some similarities between echinoderms and mollusks? What are some differences? Which group do you think is more complex? Explain.

Insects in Flight

Like a helicopter, a dragonfly can fly straight up or straight down. It can move to the right or to the left. It can glide forward or backward or simply hover in the air. And it can land on a lily pad in a pond without causing even the slightest ripple. It can reach speeds of 40 kilometers per hour and then stop on a dime.

As you can imagine, these amazing insects easily run circles around the best human-designed aircraft. For this reason, one group of researchers has been studying dragonflies to learn some of their secrets of *aerodynamics*. Aerodynamics is the study of the forces acting on an object (an airplane or a dragonfly) as it moves through the air.

One of the first goals of the researchers was to determine the lift that a dragonfly could produce. Lift is the force produced by the motion of a wing through the air. Lift is what gives an airplane the ability to climb into the air and hold itself upright during flight. Using a tiny instrument that detects small forces, researchers measured the lift generated by several species of dragonflies. They discovered that dragonflies produce three times the lift for their mass. (The mass of a dragonfly is only about one seventh the mass of a dime!)

How can dragonflies perform this feat? Researchers discovered that dragonflies twist their wings on the downward stroke. This twisting action creates tiny whirlwinds on the top surfaces of the wings. This action moves air quickly over the wings' upper surfaces, lowering air pressure there and providing incredible lift.

By applying the aerodynamic principles of dragonfly flight to airplanes, scientists may soon be able to design and build more efficient airplanes. Of course, these future airplanes will never be able to bend or flex their wings as a dragonfly does. But they may be able to take off more easily, turn faster, and touch down on tiny landing fields.

Laboratory Investigation

Investigating Isopod Environments

Problem

What type of environment do isopods (pill bugs) prefer?

Materials *(per group)*

collecting jar	aluminum foil
10 isopods	paper towels
shoe box with a lid	masking tape

Procedure

1. With the collecting jar, gather some isopods. They are usually found under loose bricks or logs. Observe the characteristics of the isopods.

2. Line the inside of the shoe box with aluminum foil.

3. Place 2 paper towels side by side in the bottom of the shoe box. Tape them down. Place a strip of masking tape between the paper towels.

4. Moisten only the paper towel on the left side of the box.

5. Place 10 isopods on the masking tape. Then place the lid on the shoe box and leave the box undisturbed for 5 minutes.

6. During the 5-minute period, predict whether the isopods will prefer the moist paper towel or the dry paper towel.

7. After 5 minutes, open the lid and quickly count the number of isopods on the dry paper towel, on the moist paper towel, and on the masking tape. Record your observations in a data table.

8. Repeat steps 5 through 7 two more times. Be sure to place the isopods on the masking tape at the start of each trial. Record the results in the data table.

9. After you have completed the three trials, determine the average number of isopods found on the dry paper towel, on the moist paper towel, and on the masking tape. Record this information in the data table. Record your average results in a class data table on the chalkboard.

Observations

1. What characteristics of isopods did you observe?

2. Where were the isopods when you opened the lid of the box? Was your prediction correct?

3. Were there variables in the experiment that could have affected the outcome? If so, what were they?

4. What was the control in this experiment?

5. How did your results compare with the class results?

Analysis and Conclusions

1. Based on your observations of their characteristics, into which phylum of invertebrates would you classify isopods? Into which group within that phylum would you place isopods?

2. From the class results, what conclusions can you draw about the habitats preferred by isopods? Give reasons for your answers.

3. What was the purpose of the masking tape in the investigation?

4. Why did you perform the investigation three times?

5. **On Your Own**   Design another investigation in which you test the following hypothesis: Isopods prefer dark environments to light environments. Be sure to include a variable and a control.

Summarizing Key Concepts

2–1 Arthropods: The "Joint-Footed" Animals

▲ Arthropods have an exoskeleton, a segmented body, and jointed appendages. An exoskeleton is a rigid outer covering.

▲ The process by which arthropods shed their exoskeleton as they grow is molting.

▲ Athropods include crustaceans, centipedes and millipedes, arachnids, and insects.

▲ A crustacean has a hard exoskeleton, two pairs of antennae, and mouthparts used for crushing and grinding food.

▲ Centipedes have one pair of legs in each body segment; millipedes have two pairs of legs in each body segment.

▲ The bodies of arachnids are divided into a head and chest part and an abdomen. Arachnids have four pairs of legs.

2–2 Insects: The Most Numerous Arthropods

▲ Insects have three body parts—head, chest, and abdomen—and three pairs of legs.

▲ The dramatic change in form an insect undergoes as it develops is called metamorphosis. There are two types of metamorphosis: complete and incomplete.

▲ During complete metamorphosis, insects go through a four-stage process: egg, larva, pupa, and adult.

▲ During incomplete metamorphosis, young insects looking very much like the adults hatch from eggs.

▲ Some species of insects give off extremely powerful chemicals called pheromones that attract either males or females.

2–3 Echinoderms: The "Spiny-Skinned" Animals

▲ Invertebrates with rough, spiny skin; an internal skeleton; a five-part body; a water vascular system; and tube feet are called echinoderms.

▲ Members of the phylum Echinodermata include starfishes, sea cucumbers, sea lilies, sea urchins, and sand dollars.

Reviewing Key Terms

Define each term in a complete sentence.

2–1 Arthropods: The "Joint-Footed" Animals
exoskeleton
molting

2–2 Insects: The Most Numerous Arthropods
metamorphosis
larva
pupa
pheromone

2–3 Echinoderms: The "Spiny-Skinned" Animals
water vascular system
tube foot

Chapter Review

Content Review

Multiple Choice

Choose the letter of the answer that best completes each statement.

1. Which is a characteristic of all arthropods?
   a. spiny skin   c. gills
   b. exoskeleton   d. backbone
2. Crustaceans obtain oxygen from the
   water through
   a. book lungs.
   b. water vascular systems.
   c. gills.
   d. air tubes.
3. Which is an example of a crustacean?
   a. sea urchin   c. grasshopper
   b. shrimp   d. scorpion
4. How many pairs of legs do millipedes
   have per body segment?
   a. 100   c. 1
   b. 2   d. 1000
5. In which stage of metamorphosis is an
   insect wrapped in a cocoon?
   a. egg   c. pupa
   b. larva   d. adult

6. Which invertebrate produces silk?
   a. lobster   c. mite
   b. spider   d. sand dollar
7. Which group includes animals that can
   fly?
   a. arachnids   c. crustaceans
   b. echinoderms d. insects
8. Which is an example of a defense
   mechanism in insects?
   a. molting
   b. camouflage
   c. pheromone production
   d. metamorphosis
9. Starfishes belong to a group of invertebrates called
   a. crustaceans. c. arachnids.
   b. arthropods.   d. echinoderms.
10. Which group of invertebrates have tube
    feet?
    a. echinoderms c. millipedes
    b. crustaceans d. arachnids

True or False

If the statement is true, write "true." If it is false, change the underlined word or words to make the statement true.

1. Arthropods have a rigid outer covering
   called an <u>exoskeleton</u>.
2. <u>Crustacean</u> means joint footed.
3. <u>Crabs</u> have <u>book lungs</u>.
4. Spiders are <u>insects</u>.
5. Mites are <u>arachnids</u>.
6. Insects have <u>three</u> pairs of legs.
7. A caterpillar is an example of a <u>larva</u>.
8. <u>Starfishes</u> have a five-part body.

Concept Mapping

Complete the following concept map for Section 2–1. Refer to pages C6–C7 to construct a concept map for the entire chapter.

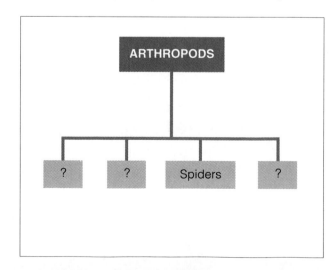

Concept Mastery

Discuss each of the following in a brief paragraph.

1. What are some advantages of having an exoskeleton? What are some disadvantages?
2. Compare complete and incomplete metamorphosis.
3. Describe the different respiratory organs that are used by arthropods.
4. Describe the different types of arthropod appendages.
5. Compare millipedes and centipedes.
6. What is the function of tube feet?
7. How do starfishes move?
8. Why are arthropods the most numerous phylum of animals?
9. What role do pheromones have in the lives of insects?
10. Explain why arthropods undergo molting.
11. Describe the functions that a worker bee, a queen bee, and a male bee have in the hive.

Critical Thinking and Problem Solving

Use the skills you have developed in this chapter to complete each of the following.

1. **Making charts** Construct a chart in which you list the groups in the phyla Arthropoda and Echinodermata, the major characteristics of the group, and three animals from each group.
2. **Classifying objects** Your friend said he found a dead insect with two body parts and eight legs. Is this possible? Explain.
3. **Making generalizations** In what ways are insects beneficial to humans?
4. **Applying concepts** The makers of horror movies invent gigantic insects that terrorize human beings. Why is it impossible for such insects to exist?
5. **Relating concepts** Insects are often described as the most successful group of animals. What characteristics of insects could account for this description?
6. **Applying technology** Pesticides are chemicals used to kill harmful insects. Describe some advantages and disadvantages of pesticide use.
7. **Using the writing process** Observe an insect such as a bee or an ant for 15 minutes. Then write a short story describing what it would be like to be one of these animals.

Fishes and Amphibians

Guide for Reading

After you read the following sections, you will be able to

3–1 What Is a Vertebrate?

- Describe the characteristics of vertebrates.
- Compare warmblooded and coldblooded vertebrates.

3–2 Fishes

- Identify the three groups of fishes and give an example of each.

3–3 Amphibians

- Describe the main characteristics of amphibians.
- Explain how metamorphosis occurs in frogs.

A sea horse is truly an unusual animal. It has the arching neck and head of a horse, the grasping tail of a monkey, and the color-changing power of a chameleon. It has eyes that move independently of each other, so that while one looks under water the other scans the surface. As if all this were not remarkable enough, sea horses have one more interesting feature: male sea horses, not female sea horses, give birth to baby sea horses!

If you look closely at the photograph on the opposite page, you can see the tails of a few baby sea horses sticking out of their father's pouch. A male sea horse bears the young. A female sea horse deposits eggs in a male sea horse's kangaroolike pouch, where they are fertilized and then cared for by the male sea horse. A few weeks later, the first baby sea horse is born, then another and another. The process continues until hundreds of tiny sea horses have emerged.

It may surprise you to learn that sea horses are actually fishes. Yes, fishes—complete with gills and fins. In the pages that follow, you will discover more about other fascinating fishes. You will also learn about the distant relatives of fishes: the amphibians.

Journal *Activity*

You and Your World Visit a supermarket and find out what kinds of fishes are available as food. In your journal, make a list of these fishes. Then choose one fish from your list and find a recipe for preparing it. Copy the recipe into your journal. Then, with the help of an adult, try it out.

◀ *A male sea horse giving birth to live young*

Guide for Reading

Focus on these questions as you read.

- *What are the main characteristics of vertebrates?*
- *What are three characteristics of chordates?*

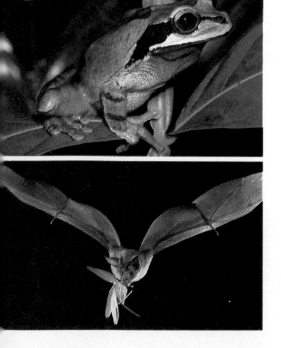

Figure 3–1 *Vertebrates are animals that have a vertebral column. Examples of vertebrates include the frog and the bat. To what phylum do vertebrates belong?*

3–1 What Is a Vertebrate?

What do trout, frogs, snakes, turtles, robins, bats, and humans have in common? The answer to this question is that all these animals are **vertebrates. A vertebrate is an animal that has a backbone, or a vertebral column.** The vertebral column of a vertebrate is important because it protects the spinal cord, which runs through the center of the backbone. The spinal cord is the connection between a vertebrate's well-developed brain and the nerves that carry information to and from every part of its body.

The vertebral column makes up part of a vertebrate's endoskeleton, or internal skeleton. (Remember, the prefix *endo-* means inner.) The endoskeleton provides support and helps to give shape to the body of a vertebrate. One important advantage of an endoskeleton is that it is made of living tissue, so it grows as the animal grows. This is quite unlike the exoskeleton of an arthropod, which is made of nonliving material and has to be shed as the animal grows.

All vertebrates belong to the phylum Chordata (kor-DAT-uh). Members of the phylum Chordata are known as chordates. **At some time during their lives, all chordates have three important characteristics: a nerve cord, a notochord, and a throat with gill slits.** The nerve cord is a hollow tube located near the animal's back. Just beneath the nerve cord is the notochord. The notochord is a long, flexible supporting rod that runs through part of the animal's body. In most vertebrates, the notochord is replaced by the vertebral column. The gill slits are paired structures located in the throat (or pharynx) region that connect the throat cavity with the outside environment. Water easily flows over the **gills,** allowing oxygen to pass into the blood vessels in the gills and carbon dioxide to pass out into the water. Gills are feathery structures through which water-dwelling animals, such as fishes, breathe.

Figure 3–2 *In addition to illustrating one hypothesis about the evolutionary relationships among vertebrate groups, this phylogenetic tree also shows approximately when certain characteristics occurred. When did four limbs appear?* ▶

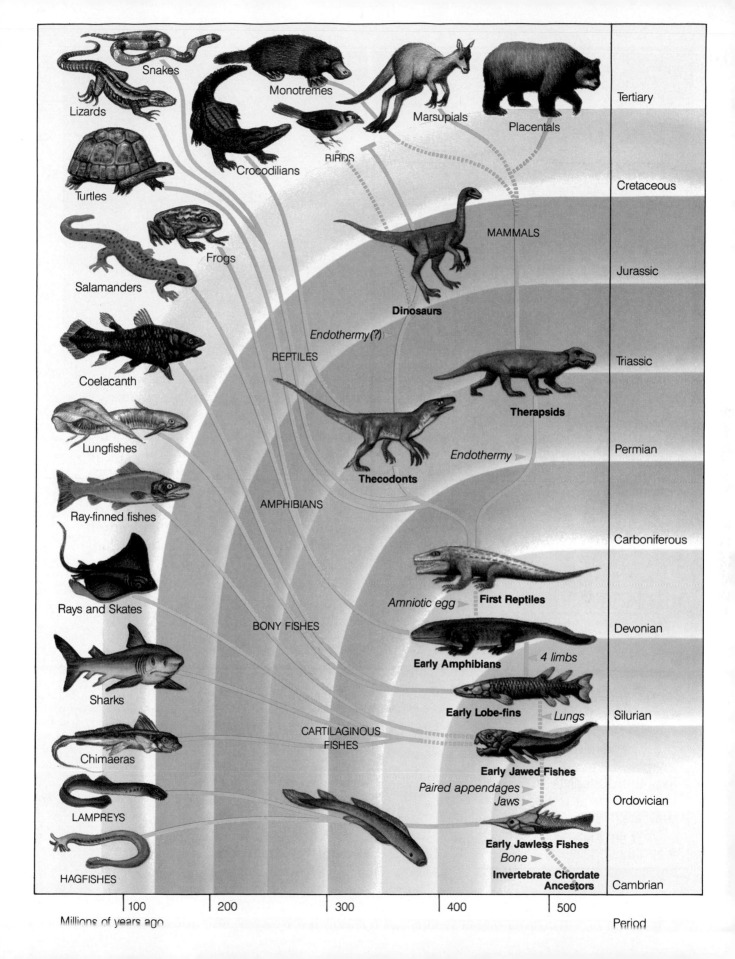

Snakes

Monotremes

Marsupials

Tertiary

Lizards

Crocodilians

BIRDS

Placentals

Turtles

MAMMALS

Cretaceous

Salamanders

Frogs

Dinosaurs

Jurassic

Coelacanth

REPTILES

Endothermy (?)

Therapsids

Triassic

Lungfishes

Thecodonts

Endothermy

Permian

Ray-finned fishes

AMPHIBIANS

Carboniferous

Rays and Skates

Amniotic egg

First Reptiles

BONY FISHES

Devonian

Early Amphibians

4 limbs

Sharks

Early Lobe-fins

Lungs

Silurian

Chimaeras

CARTILAGINOUS
FISHES

Early Jawed Fishes

LAMPREYS

Paired appendages

Jaws

Ordovician

Early Jawless Fishes

HAGFISHES

Bone

Invertebrate Chordate
Ancestors

Cambrian

100   200   300   400   500

Millions of years ago

Period

Figure 3–3 *Vertebrates may be either coldblooded or warmblooded. The iguana, which is a reptile, is a coldblooded vertebrate. The polar bear, which is a mammal, is a warmblooded vertebrate.*

There are eight groups of vertebrates within the phylum Chordata. Of the eight groups, six are **coldblooded** and two are **warmblooded.** Coldblooded animals (more correctly called ectotherms), such as fishes, amphibians, and reptiles, do not produce much internal heat. Thus they must rely on their environment for the heat they need. Warmblooded animals (endotherms), such as birds and mammals, maintain their body temperatures internally as a result of all the chemical reactions that occur within their cells. In other words, coldblooded animals have body temperatures that change somewhat with the temperature of their surroundings; warmblooded animals maintain a constant body temperature.

ACTIVITY

DOING

Tunicates

Tunicates are members of the phylum Chordata. Using reference materials in the library, find out about these animals. Present your findings to the class in an oral report. Include a drawing of a tunicate.

Why are these animals classified as chordates?

3–1 Section Review

1. What are the main characteristics of vertebrates?
2. List three characteristics of chordates.
3. Compare a coldblooded animal and a warmblooded animal.
4. What are gills?

Critical Thinking—*Applying Concepts*

5. Are you warmblooded or coldblooded? Explain your answer.

3–2 Fishes

About 540 million years ago the first fishes appeared in the Earth's oceans. These fishes were strange-looking animals, indeed! They had no jaws, and their bodies were covered by bony plates instead of scales. And although they had fins, the fins were not like those of modern-day fishes. But these early fishes were the first animals to have vertebral columns. They were the first vertebrates to have evolved.

Despite these differences, there was something special about these animals—something that would group them with the many kinds of fishes that were to follow millions of years later. **Fishes are water-dwelling vertebrates that are characterized by scales, fins, and throats with gill slits.** It is important to note, however, that not all fishes have all these characteristics. For example, sturgeons, paddlefishes, and sea horses have no scales at all on most of their body. And although most fishes have fins, the fins vary greatly in structure and function. Some fishes have paired fins, whereas others have single fins. Some fishes use their fins to help them remain upright. Other fishes use their fins to help them steer and stop. The side-to-side movement of large tail fins helps most fishes to move through the water. However, all fishes have gill slits.

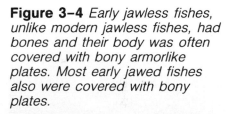

Figure 3–4 *Early jawless fishes, unlike modern jawless fishes, had bones and their body was often covered with bony armorlike plates. Most early jawed fishes also were covered with bony plates.*

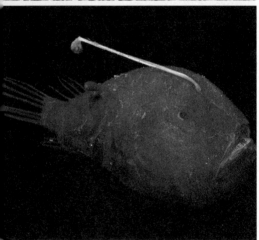

Figure 3-5 *Fishes have developed special structures that enable them to catch or eat a great variety of foods. The parrotfish (top) uses its "beak" to bite off chunks of coral. The oyster toadfish (center) relies on its ability to blend in with its surroundings to catch its prey. The seadevil (bottom) uses its bright lure to attract unsuspecting victims.*

As a group, fishes eat just about everything—from microscopic algae to worms to dead fish. The parrotfish even eats coral! Fishes have developed special structures that enable them to catch or eat the great variety of foods upon which they feed. Swordfishes are thought to slash their way through large groups of fishes and then return to devour the wounded or dead prey. Toad fishes rely on their ability to blend in with their surroundings to catch their prey. And angler fishes have wormlike lures that they dangle in front of their prey.

Like all vertebrates, fishes have a closed circulatory system. A closed circulatory system is one in which the blood is contained within blood vessels. In fishes, the blood travels through the blood vessels in a single loop—from the heart to the gills to the rest of the body and back to the heart. The excretory system of fishes consists of tubelike kidneys that filter nitrogen-containing wastes from the blood. Like many other water-dwelling animals, most fishes get rid of the nitrogen-containing wastes in the form of ammonia.

Fishes have a fairly well-developed nervous system. Almost all fishes have sense organs that collect information about their environment. Most fishes that are active in daylight have eyes with color vision almost as good as yours. Those fishes that are active at night or that live in murky water have large eyes with big pupils. Do you know what this adaptation enables them to do?

Many fishes have keen senses of smell and taste. For example, sharks can detect the presence of one drop of blood in 115 liters of sea water! Although most fishes cannot hear sounds well, they can detect faint currents and vibrations in the water through a "distant-touch" system. As a fish moves, its distant-touch system responds to changes in the movement of the water, thus enabling the fish to detect prey or to avoid objects in its path.

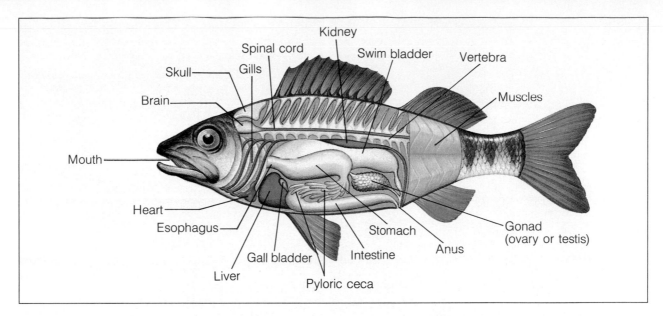

Figure 3–6 The internal organs of a typical bony fish are shown here. What structures enable fishes to breathe?

In most species of fishes, males and females are separate individuals. The males produce sperm, and the females produce eggs. There are, however, a number of fish species that are born males but develop into females. Others begin their lives as females and then change into males. Whatever the case, few fishes function as both a male and a female at the same time.

Of the many fishes that lay eggs, most have **external fertilization.** External fertilization is the process in which a sperm joins with an egg outside the body. Certain egg-laying fishes have **internal fertilization.** Internal fertilization is the process in which a sperm joins with an egg inside the body. Of the fishes that have internal fertilization, some—such as sharks and rays—lay fertilized eggs. In other fishes that have internal fertilization, the eggs develop inside the female's body. In this case, each developing fish receives food either directly from the female or indirectly from a yolk sac attached to its body. When all the food in its yolk sac is used up, the young fish is born.

Figure 3–7 Fishes have well-developed sense organs. For example, the eyes of the four-eyed fish, or quatro ojos, are each divided horizontally into two sections (right). The upper eyes are used to see above the water, whereas the lower eyes are used to see below the water. The "distant touch" system of the rainbow trout, which appears as a series of tiny dots in the pink stripe (left), detects movements in the water.

Figure 3–8 *Although all sharks have internal fertilization, the young of some sharks, such as the swell shark (left), develop outside the female's body. In grunions (top right), fertilization and development of young occur outside the female's body. In guppies (bottom right), fertilization and development of young occur inside the female's body.*

Many fishes (including some you can keep in an aquarium) have interesting mating behaviors. For example, male guppies dance in front of female guppies to get their attention. The bright red and blue body of a male three-spined stickleback serves to let female sticklebacks know where his nest is, as well as to warn other males to keep away.

The correct scientific classification of fishes is quite complicated. Thus, in this textbook fishes are placed into three main groups. These groups are the jawless fishes, the cartilaginous (KAHRT'l-aj-uh-nuhs) fishes, and the bony fishes.

Jawless Fishes

Jawless fishes are the most primitive of all fishes. They are so primitive, in fact, that in addition to lacking jaws, they also lack scales and paired fins. Something else makes jawless fishes unusual. To find out what it is, hold one of your ears between your fingers and move it back and forth a few times. How are you able to perform this action? The answer is that your ear contains a flexible material called cartilage. The entire skeleton of jawless fishes is made of cartilage. Jawless fishes are vertebrates that have no bone at all. (Later in this section you will read about another group of fishes that also contain no bone.)

The only support the eellike bodies have is a notochord. As you might expect, jawless fishes are really flexible.

To see examples of the only two species of jawless fishes still alive—lampreys and hagfishes—look at Figure 3–9. Notice that a lamprey looks like an eel with a suction-cup mouth at one end. This suction-cup mouth, which is surrounded by horny teeth, is extremely efficient. Using its mouth, a lamprey attaches itself to a fish such as a trout (or sometimes a whale or a porpoise) and scrapes away at the fish's skin with its teeth and rough tongue. Then it sucks up the tissues and other fluids of its victim.

The skin of a lamprey is covered with glands that release a slippery, sticky substance called mucus (MYOO-kuhs). This mucus is toxic, or poisonous, and it probably discourages larger fishes from eating lampreys.

The other jawless fishes—the hagfishes—are considered the most primitive vertebrates alive today. The most obvious feature of a hagfish's wormlike body is the four to six short tentacles that surround its nostrils and mouth. The tentacles are used as organs of touch.

A hagfish feeds on dead or dying fishes by tearing out pieces of the fish with a tongue that has teethlike structures. If the fish is large, a hagfish will twist its own body into a knot so that it can thrust itself into the fish with extra power. In no time, the hagfish will be completely inside the prey fish. The ability to twist itself into a knot also enables a hagfish to evade capture, especially when this action is accompanied by the release of a sticky, slimy material from pores located along the sides of its body. A single hagfish can release so much slime that if it is placed in a pail of sea water, it can turn the entire contents of the pail into slime.

Cartilaginous Fishes

When you think of sharks, you probably think of large fast-swimming vicious predators. Although this is true of some sharks, it is not true of most. For the most part, sharks prefer to be left alone.

Sharks—along with rays, skates, and two rare fishes called sawfishes and chimaeras (kigh-MIHR-uhz)—are cartilaginous fishes. Like jawless fishes,

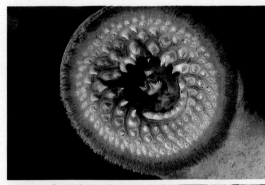

Figure 3–9 *Modern jawless fishes include only two species: the lampreys (top) and the hagfishes (bottom). In addition to being jawless, what are some other characteristics of jawless fishes?*

ACTIVITY
DISCOVERING

The Invasion of the Lamprey

The completion of the St. Lawrence Seaway accidentally introduced lampreys into the Great Lakes. Using reference materials in the library, find out what effects lampreys have had on fishes already living there. Construct a chart that indicates what fishes lived in the Great Lakes before and after the arrival of lampreys.

■ What might have been done to prevent this from happening?

Figure 3–10 *The southern stingray (left), big skate (bottom right), and sawfish (top right) are examples of cartilaginous fishes.*

ACTIVITY

DOING

Observing a Fish

1. Obtain a preserved fish from your teacher and place it in a tray.

2. Hold the fish in your hands and observe it. Note the size, shape, and color of the fish. Also note the number and location of the fins.

3. Draw a diagram of the fish and label as many structures as you can.

4. Locate the fish's gill cover. Lift it up and examine the gills with a hand lens.

To which group of fishes does your fish belong?

cartilaginous fishes have skeletons made of cartilage. Most of them also have toothlike scales covering their bodies. The toothlike scales are the reason why the skin of a shark feels as rough as sandpaper. Most of the more than 2000 types of sharks have torpedo-shaped bodies, curved tails, and rounded snouts with a mouth underneath.

The most obvious feature of a shark is its teeth. At any one time, a fish-eating shark will have 3000 very long teeth arranged in six to twenty rows in its mouth. In most sharks, the first one or two rows of teeth are used for feeding. The remaining rows contain replacement teeth, with the newest teeth at the back. As a tooth in the front row breaks or is worn down, it falls out. When this happens, a replacement tooth moves forward in a kind of conveyor-belt system. In its lifetime, a single shark may go through more than 20,000 teeth! Not all sharks, however, have the long teeth characteristic of fish-eating sharks. Sharks that eat mollusks and crustaceans have flattened teeth that help them to crush the shells of their prey.

Unlike sharks, the bodies of skates and rays are as flat as pancakes. For this reason, skates and rays are sometimes called pancake sharks. These cartilaginous fishes have two large, broad fins that stick out from their sides. They beat these fins to move through the water, much as a bird beats its wings to fly through the air. Rays and skates often lie on the ocean bottom, where they hide by using their fins to cover their bodies with sand. When an unsuspecting fish or invertebrate comes near, the hidden skate or ray is ready to attack. Some rays have a poisonous spine at the end of their long, thin tail, which they use for defense rather than for catching prey. Other rays, appropriately called electric rays, have a specialized organ in their head that can discharge about 200 volts of electricity to stun and capture prey. Although 200 volts may not sound like a lot, you only need 120 volts to power almost everything in your home!

Bony Fishes

If you have ever eaten a flounder or a trout, you know why such fishes are called bony fishes. Their skeleton is made of hard bones, many of which are quite small and sharp. Some bony fishes, such as tunas, travel in groups called schools. Because of this schooling behavior, these fishes can be caught in large numbers at one time by people in fishing boats.

Although all bony fishes have paired fins, the shape of the paired fins varies considerably. Most bony fishes have fins supported by a number of long bones called rays. Thus these fishes are called ray-finned fishes. Perches and sea horses are two examples of ray-finned bony fishes. Other fishes have fins with fleshy bases supported by leglike bones. These fishes are known as lobe-finned fishes. Coelacanths (SEE-luh-kanths) are the only living species of lobe-finned bony fishes.

Another characteristic of bony fishes is that they have **swim bladders.** A swim bladder is a gas-filled sac that gives bony fishes buoyancy, or the ability to float in water. By inflating or deflating its swim bladder, a fish can float at different levels in the water.

There are many kinds of bony fishes, some of which have developed remarkable adaptations to life in water. For example, an electric eel can produce jolts of electricity up to 650 volts for use in defending itself or in stunning its prey. A remora uses its sucker to attach itself to sharks or other large fishes, feeding on bits of food they leave behind. Can you see why a remora is sometimes called a shark sucker?

Figure 3–11 *The sand tiger shark (top) shows one of the most noticeable characteristics of sharks: enormous numbers of teeth. The flattened body of the wobbegong, or carpet shark (center), and of the blue-spotted stingray (bottom) is an adaptation to life on the bottom of the ocean.*

Activity Bank

To Float or Not to Float?, p.161

Figure 3–12 *Bony fishes come in a wide variety of shapes and colors. The queen angelfish (bottom left) has a flattened, highly colorful body. The moray eel (top right) has a narrow, snakelike body. The body of the glass, or ghost, catfish (top left) is almost transparent except for its head and bones. Unlike its ancestors, which lived more than 70 million years ago, the present-day coelacanth (bottom right) still has its paired lobed fins.*

ACTIVITY

READING

A Fish Story

You may want to read a wonderful novel about an old man and his struggle with nature as he pursues a large fish. The novel is entitled *The Old Man and the Sea,* and the author is Ernest Hemingway.

Another fish that has developed an interesting adaptation to its surroundings is the flounder. All adult flounders are bottom-dwelling fishes. However, a flounder's eggs, which contain oil droplets, float at or near the surface of the water. When a young flounder begins its life, it does so as a normally shaped fish with one eye on each side of its head and a horizontal mouth. But as the young fish develops into an adult, one of its eyes moves to the other side of the head and the mouth twists. Because it does not have a swim bladder, the adult flounder eventually sinks to the ocean's bottom and lies permanently on one side—usually, the blind side. The fact that the flounder has its eyes and mouth on the same side of its body makes it easier for the flounder to see what is going on around it and to take in food. Lying on its side, a flounder is vulnerable to attack from its predators. But another adaptation—the ability to change the color of its body so that it matches the color of the ocean bottom—gives it protection from its predators.

Fishes that live in the depths of the ocean also have developed special adaptations. Lantern fishes, which live at depths of 300 to 700 meters, have light-emitting organs that attract prey. Other deep-sea fishes have huge eyes that help them to see better in the dark depths of the ocean.

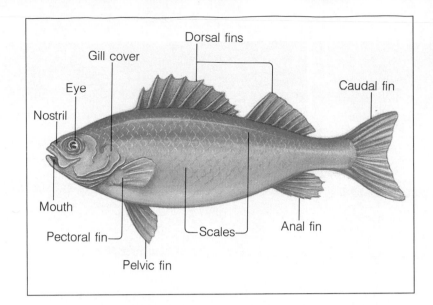

Figure 3-13 *Although this diagram shows the different types of fins that may be present in fishes, not every kind of fish possesses all these fins.*

Eye
Nostril
Gill cover
Dorsal fins
Caudal fin
Mouth
Pectoral fin
Pelvic fin
Scales
Anal fin

Still other fishes have developed adaptations that allow them to come out of water and spend some time on land. For example, mudskippers spend a lot of time using their fins to walk or "skip" on land at low tide. During these periods, a mudskipper can breathe air through its skin, as well as exchange oxygen for carbon dioxide in its mouth and throat. Another type of fish that can live on land for a short time is the African lungfish. When the swamp in which it lives dries up, an African lungfish burrows into the soft mud and becomes inactive until the rains come. When water is again available, the lungfish emerges.

Figure 3-14 *Bony fishes have developed many interesting adaptations to their life in water. The electric eel can discharge small amounts of electricity to protect itself from predators (bottom right). The remora, or sharksucker, has a suctionlike disk that it uses to "hitch a ride" on a shark (top right). The long, graceful rays of the lionfish contain poisonous spines, which help keep its predators away (left).*

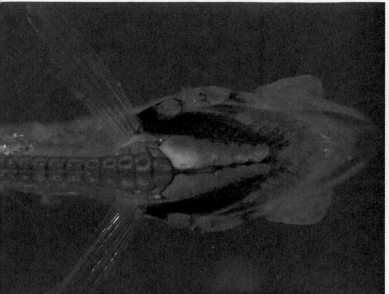

Figure 3–15 *Some bony fishes, such as the lantern fish, have light organs that enable them to live in the dark depths of the ocean. Other bony fishes, such as the African lungfish, have developed adaptations that allow them to live on land for short periods of time.*

3–2 Section Review

1. What are the main characteristics of fishes?
2. List the three groups of fishes and give an example of each.
3. Compare internal and external fertilization.
4. What is the function of a swim bladder?

Connection—*Ecology*
5. How would the Atlantic salmon be affected if its freshwater streams became badly polluted?

Guide for Reading

Focus on these questions as you read.

▶ *What are the main characteristics of amphibians?*

▶ *What are some examples of amphibians?*

3–3 Amphibians

The forests of Colombia in South America are home to the Choco Indian tribe. There, the Indians continue a centuries-old tradition of hunting deer, monkeys, and even jaguars with poisoned arrows. In order to do so, the Indians must first capture a number of special kinds of frogs that live in the area. The Indians roast the frogs over a fire so that the poison drips from the skin. The poison is collected in pots and then smeared onto the tips of the arrows. The poison is so powerful that 0.00001 gram is enough to kill a person! So little poison is needed on the tip of an arrow that a 2.5-centimeter frog can produce enough to cover 50 arrows. Appropriately, this frog is known as the arrow-poison frog.

Arrow-poison frogs are members of the second group of coldblooded vertebrates: the amphibians. Amphibians first appeared on Earth about 360 million years ago. They are thought to have evolved from lobe-finned bony fishes that had lungs—fishes similar to a modern coelacanth.

The word amphibian means double life. And most amphibians do live a double life. **Amphibians are vertebrates that are fishlike and that breathe through gills when immature. They live on land and breathe through lungs and moist skin as adults. Their skin also contains many glands, and their bodies lack scales and claws.** Naturally, there are exceptions. Some amphibians spend their entire lives on land. Others live their entire lives in water. But it is safe to say that most amphibians live in water for the first part of their lives and on land in moist areas as adults.

Why must most amphibians live in moist areas? One reason is that their eggs lack hard outer shells. If not deposited in water, such eggs would dry out. Another reason why adult amphibians cannot stray too far from a moist area is that in addition to breathing through lungs, they also breathe through

Figure 3–16 *There are three main groups of amphibians: frogs and toads, salamanders and newts, and legless amphibians. The red-eyed tree frog (left) can climb trees as well as hop. The red-bellied newt (top right) keeps its tail throughout its life. The burrowing caecilian (bottom right) preys on small animals it meets as it tunnels through the ground. What are the main characteristics of all amphibians?*

their skin. And in order to do so, the skin must remain moist. If the skin dries out, most amphibians will suffocate.

The circulatory system of adult amphibians forms a double loop. One loop transports oxygen-poor and oxygen-rich blood back and forth between the heart and the lungs. The other loop transports

Figure 3–17 *The major internal organs of a frog are shown in these two diagrams. Which organs enable the frog to breathe?*

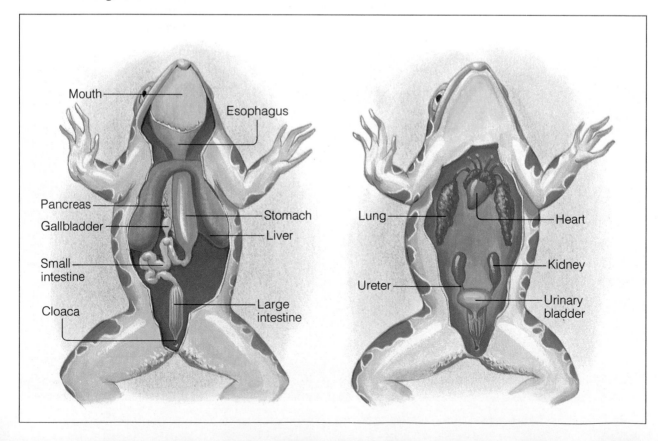

Figure 3–18 *This diagram shows what amphibians may have looked like 270 million years ago. What characteristics do they have in common with modern amphibians?*

oxygen-rich and oxygen-poor blood between the heart and the rest of the body. Tadpoles, or the young of certain amphibians, have a single-loop circulatory system, as do bony fishes. In this type of system, blood travels from the heart to the gills to the rest of the body and back to the heart.

Amphibians have two oval-shaped kidneys that filter wastes from the blood. The nitrogen-containing wastes are in the form of urine, which is then transported by tubes out of the body.

The nervous system and the sense organs are well-developed in amphibians. Large eyes, which bulge out from the sides of the head, provide sharp vision. A transparent membrane protects the eyes from drying out while the animal is on land and from being damaged while the animal is under water.

Many amphibians reproduce by external fertilization. In frogs, for example, a female releases eggs that are then fertilized by a male. After a sticky, transparent jelly forms around the fertilized eggs, the eggs become attached to underwater plants. In a few weeks the eggs hatch into tadpoles, or polliwogs. A tadpole has gills to breathe under water and feeds on plants. Eventually, the process of **metamorphosis** (meht-uh-MOR-fuh-sihs), or the series of dramatic changes in body form in an amphibian's life cycle, begins. During this process, the tadpole undergoes remarkable changes. It loses its tail and develops two

ACTIVITY

DOING

A Frog Jumping Contest

1. Find a flat surface that measures 1.5 m x 1.5 m. Draw four concentric circles with diameters of 30 cm, 60 cm, 90 cm, and 120 cm on the surface.

2. Place a frog in the middle of the innermost circle. Measure how far the frog jumps. Record the distance.

3. Repeat step 2 two more times. Find the average distance your frog jumps.

How far did your frog jump? Which legs do frogs use for jumping—the front legs or the hind legs? To which group of vertebrates do frogs belong? Explain your answer.

pairs of legs. Its gills begin to disappear, and its lungs complete their development. The tadpole is now an adult frog, ready for life on land.

Not all amphibians lay eggs and have external fertilization. Of the many amphibians that have internal fertilization, some lay fertilized eggs. In others, the fertilized eggs develop inside the body of a female, where they receive their food directly from the female or indirectly from a yolk sac. Amphibians have varying ways of caring for their young. Some frogs carry their young in their mouth or in their stomach. Others have special structures on their back in which their young develop.

Figure 3–19 *Like most amphibians, frogs live in water for the first part of their life and on land in moist areas as an adult. Frog eggs are fertilized externally (top right) and generally develop in water (center left). Soon the fertilized eggs develop into young with tails (center right) and then hatch into tadpoles (bottom left). Gradually, the tadpoles grow limbs and begin to lose their tails (bottom right) as they develop into adults. What is this process called?*

Frogs and Toads

Have you ever wondered what happens to frogs and toads in the winter when the temperature falls? Frogs and toads, like all amphibians, are unable to move to warmer climates. They do, however, survive the cold. Frogs often bury themselves beneath the muddy floor of a lake during the winter. Toads dig through dry ground below the frost line. Then these amphibians go into a winter sleep called hibernation. During hibernation, all body activities slow down so that the animal can live on food stored in its body. The small amount of oxygen needed during hibernation passes through the amphibian's skin as it sleeps. Once warmer weather comes, the frog or toad awakens. If you live in the country, you can usually tell when this happens. The night suddenly becomes filled with the familiar peeps, squeaks, chirps, and grunts that male frogs and toads use to attract female mates.

Although frogs and toads appear similar in shape, you can discover one difference merely by touching

ACTIVITY READING

Jumping Frogs

Mark Twain, whose real name was Samuel Langhorne Clemens, wrote a humorous short story about the jumping ability of a frog named Daniel Webster. The title of the short story is "The Notorious Jumping Frog of Calaveras County."

Figure 3–20 *Frogs and toads have developed adaptations that help them escape their predators. The tomato toad (bottom right) has glands behind its eyes that contain poison. The Amazon horned toad (bottom left) is almost invisible as it hides among dead leaves. The European tree frog (top) has long, muscular legs that enable it to quickly leap away from its enemies.*

them. Frogs have a smooth, moist skin. Toads have skin that is drier and is usually covered with small wartlike bumps. In many toads, the bumps behind the eyes contain a poisonous liquid, which the toad releases when attacked. A great cane toad can squirt a jet of poison at an attacker almost a meter away. The attacking animal quickly becomes sick and may even die.

If there is one thing most people know about adult frogs and toads, it is that they are excellent jumpers. The main reason for this is that the hind legs of a frog or a toad are much larger than the front legs. It is these powerful hind legs that enable these animals to jump so well and that help them to escape from their enemies.

Salamanders and Newts

Salamanders and newts are amphibians that keep their tails throughout their lives. Like frogs and toads, these animals have two pairs of legs. But their hind legs are not as developed as those of a frog or a toad. Thus salamanders and newts are not able to jump.

Because they are amphibians, salamanders and newts must live in moist areas. One type of salamander, the mud puppy, lives in water all its life even though as an adult it has both lungs and gills. Like frogs and toads, salamanders and newts lay their eggs in water.

Figure 3–21 *Unlike most amphibians, salamanders and newts—such as the mud puppy (left) and red-spotted newt (right)—keep their tail throughout their life.*

3–3 Section Review

1. What are the characteristics of amphibians?
2. List some examples of amphibians.
3. Explain how amphibians live double lives.
4. Compare a tadpole with an adult frog. List at least three differences between them.

Critical Thinking—*Relating Concepts*
5. Amphibians can lay as many as 200 eggs. Why do you think it is necessary for most amphibians to produce so many eggs?

CONNECTIONS

Can Toads Cause Warts?

Have you ever been told that you can get warts by touching a toad? Contrary to superstition, touching the skin of a toad does not cause warts. Although a pair of large glands on the top of a toad's head does give off a poison that can irritate your eyes or make you ill, toads do not produce warts.

Warts—hard, rough growths on the surface of the skin—are actually caused by certain *viruses*. These viruses live in cells on the surface of the skin and do not invade the tissue underneath.

Some warts disappear as mysteriously as they appeared. Perhaps an immunity to the virus develops. An immunity is a resistance to a disease-causing organism or a harmful substance. If a wart does not go away by itself, medical attention should be sought. Under no circumstances should you try to remove a wart without medical help.

So feel free to handle toads all you want. Their wart-producing reputation is simply nonsense!

Laboratory Investigation

Designing an Aquatic Environment

Problem

What type of environment is best for guppies?

Materials *(per group)*

rectangular aquarium (15 to 20 liters)
aquarium light (optional)
gravel

metric ruler

water plants

aquarium filter

snails

guppies

aquarium cover

guppy food

thermometer

dip net

Procedure 🧪 ⊶ 🛌

1. Wash the aquarium with lukewarm water and place it on a flat surface in indirect sunlight. Do not use soap when washing the aquarium.

2. Rinse the gravel and use it to cover the bottom of the aquarium to a depth of about 3.5 cm.

3. Fill the aquarium about two-thirds full with tap water.

4. Gently place water plants into the aquarium by pushing their roots into the gravel. If you have a filter, place it in the aquarium and turn it on.

5. Add more water until the water level is about 5 cm from the top of the aquarium. Let the aquarium stand for 2 days.

6. Add the snails and guppies to the aquarium. Use one guppy and one snail for every 4 liters of water.

7. Place the cover on top of the aquarium.

8. Keep the temperature of the aquarium between 23°C and 27°C. Feed the guppies a small amount of food each day. Add tap water that has been left standing for 24 hours to the aquarium as needed. Remove any dead plants or animals.

9. Observe the aquarium every day for 2 weeks. Record your observations.

Observations

1. Do the guppies swim alone or in a school?

2. What do you see when you observe the gills of guppies?

3. Describe the reaction of guppies when food is placed in the aquarium.

4. Describe the method snails use to obtain their food.

5. Was there any growth in the water plants? How do you know?

Analysis and Conclusions

1. To what phylum of animals do snails belong? To what phylum of animals do guppies belong? How do you know?

2. How do fishes obtain oxygen?

3. What is the function of the water plants in the aquarium? The function of snails?

4. Why is it important that you do not overfeed the guppies?

5. Why did you allow the tap water to stand for 24 hours?

6. **On Your Own**   Design an experiment to determine how the aquarium would be affected by the following conditions: placing the aquarium in direct sunlight and in darkness and adding guppies.

Summarizing Key Concepts

3–1 What Is a Vertebrate?

▲ A vertebrate is an animal that has a backbone, or vertebral column. The vertebral column is part of a vertebrate's endoskeleton, or internal skeleton.

▲ All vertebrates belong to the phylum Chordata. At some time during their lives, all chordates have three important characteristics: a nerve cord, a notochord, and a throat with gill slits.

▲ Gills are feathery structures in which the exchange of the gases oxygen and carbon dioxide occurs. Fishes have gills.

▲ Coldblooded animals do not produce much heat. Thus they must rely on their environment for the heat they need.

▲ Warmblooded animals maintain their body temperatures internally as a result of the chemical reactions that occur within their cells.

3–2 Fishes

▲ Fishes are water-dwelling vertebrates that are characterized by scales, fins, and throats with gill slits.

▲ Fertilization in fishes may be external or internal. External fertilization is the process in which a sperm joins with an egg outside the body. Internal fertilization is the process in which a sperm joins with an egg inside the body.

▲ Fishes are placed into three main groups: jawless fishes, cartilaginous fishes, and bony fishes.

▲ Jawless fishes are eellike fishes that lack paired fins, scales, and a backbone.

▲ Cartilaginous fishes have a skeleton of flexible cartilage.

▲ Bony fishes have skeletons of bone. Most have swim bladders, which are gas-filled sacs that give bony fishes their buoyancy.

3–3 Amphibians

▲ Amphibians are vertebrates that are fishlike and that breathe through gills when immature. They live on land and breathe through lungs and moist skin as adults. Their skin also contains many glands, and their bodies lack scales and claws.

▲ Young amphibians have a single-loop circulatory system. Adult amphibians have a double-loop circulatory system.

▲ Fertilization in amphibians may be external or internal.

▲ Metamorphosis is a series of dramatic changes in body form in an amphibian's life cycle.

▲ As adults, frogs and toads develop lungs and legs.

▲ Salamanders and newts are amphibians with tails.

Reviewing Key Terms

Define each term in a complete sentence.

3–1 What Is a Vertebrate?
vertebrate
gill
coldblooded
warmblooded

3–2 Fishes
external fertilization
internal fertilization
swim bladder

3–3 Amphibians
metamorphosis

Chapter Review

Content Review

Multiple Choice

Choose the letter of the answer that best completes each statement.

1. All vertebrates have
   a. bony skeletons.
   b. scales.
   c. vertebral columns.
   d. exoskeletons.
2. Which is not a vertebrate?
   a. snake   c. shark
   b. earthworm   d. lizard
3. Which group of vertebrates are warm-blooded?
   a. mammals   c. amphibians
   b. fishes   d. reptiles
4. Which is best suited for life in water?
   a. toad   c. trout
   b. newt   d. frog
5. Which fish lacks jaws, scales, and paired fins?
   a. paddlefish   c. shark
   b. hagfish   d. skate

6. Which is a cartilaginous fish?
   a. electric eel   c. trout
   b. lungfish   d. ray
7. Bony fishes can float at different levels in the water because they have
   a. backbones.   c. fins.
   b. swim bladders. d. gills.
8. Amphibians must lay their eggs
   a. on land.   c. in nests.
   b. in water.   d. in shells.
9. Immature frogs breathe through their
   a. lungs.   c. gills.
   b. skin.   d. mouth.
10. Which is not an amphibian?
   a. frog   c. newt
   b. toad   d. lamprey

True or False

If the statement is true, write "true." If it is false, change the underlined word or words to make the statement true.

1. <u>Vertebrates</u> are members of the phylum Chordata.
2. All vertebrates have an <u>endoskeleton</u>.
3. The <u>cartilaginous</u> fishes are the most primitive group of fishes.
4. The lamprey is a <u>jawless</u> fish.
5. Sharks are <u>bony</u> fishes.
6. The skin of a toad is <u>drier</u> than that of a frog.
7. Adult amphibians obtain most of their oxygen through their <u>lungs</u>.
8. Newts and salamanders are <u>fishes</u> with tails.

Concept Mapping

Complete the following concept map for Section 3–1. Refer to pages C6–C7 to construct a concept map for the entire chapter.

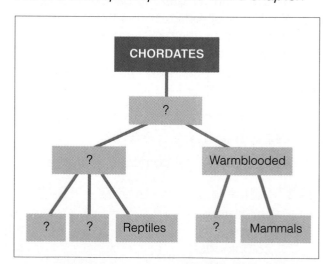

Concept Mastery

Discuss each of the following in a brief paragraph.

1. What adaptations have fishes developed that enable them to live in water?
2. Explain why amphibians must live in a moist environment.
3. Describe the main characteristics of chordates.
4. What adaptations have adult amphibians developed that allow them to live successfully on land?
5. How does a double-loop circulatory system differ from a single-loop circulatory system?
6. What is the "distant touch" system in fishes?
7. How do fishes care for their young?
8. Compare the three groups of fishes.
9. Hypothesize why those vertebrates that reproduce by internal fertilization tend to produce fewer eggs than do those animals that reproduce by external fertilization.
10. Describe metamorphosis in frogs.
11. Explain what happens to frogs and toads when they go into hibernation.

Critical Thinking and Problem Solving

Use the skills you have developed in this chapter to complete each of the following.

1. **Relating facts** Why would you never find frogs living in Antarctica?
2. **Making inferences** People who fish often use a variety of artificial lures. Explain how these lures could attract fishes.
3. **Developing a hypothesis** Some fishes have light colors on their bottom surfaces and dark colors on their top surfaces. Develop a hypothesis to explain how this coloration could be an advantage.
4. **Relating facts** When a raccoon catches a toad, it usually wipes the amphibian along the ground before eating it. Suggest a reason for this strange behavior.
5. **Applying concepts** A female bullfrog can produce as many as 25,000 eggs in a year. Explain why the Earth is not overrun with bullfrogs.
6. **Designing an experiment** Design an experiment in which you determine whether salamanders are able to detect sound. Be sure to include a variable and a control in your experiment.
7. **Using the writing process** Pretend that you received a letter from a friend who lives in another state. She has told you about a small four-legged cold-blooded vertebrate that she found. She wants to know if it is a frog or a salamander. Write a letter telling her how she can determine what her animal is.

Reptiles and Birds

4

Guide for Reading

After you read the following sections, you will be able to

4–1 Reptiles

■ Describe the adaptations that allow reptiles to live their entire lives on land.

■ Explain how reptiles carry out their major life functions.

4–2 Birds

■ Describe the characteristics of birds.

■ Discuss the ways in which birds perform their major life functions.

Imagine that you have just journeyed back in time. You step out of your time machine and enter the world of 150 million years ago.

As you look around at this strange world of the past, it becomes clear to you why this part of Earth's history is sometimes called the Age of Reptiles: Reptiles are the dominant form of life. Long-beaked reptiles soar on narrow wings in the sky above you. Porpoiselike reptiles come to the surface of the ocean for a breath of air, then dive back into the depths with a flick of their fishlike tail. On land, the reptiles known as dinosaurs roam among forests of tree ferns, conifers, and cycads. A rhinoceros-sized dinosaur with huge pointed plates on its back swishes its spike-tipped tail as you approach. Fierce meat-eating dinosaurs as tall as giraffes run swiftly on their two hind legs, pursuing a herd of plant-eating dinosaurs that are, astoundingly, even taller!

Although most of the reptiles of 150 million years ago have died out, some types have survived to the present. What are reptiles? What sorts of reptiles are alive today? Where do reptiles fit in the evolutionary tree of life? Read on and learn about reptiles and birds—living relatives of dinosaurs.

Journal *Activity*

You and Your World In your journal, list ten of the most important facts that you already know about reptiles. Make a similar list for birds. Compare your list with a friend's list and discuss any differences. After you have finished studying this chapter, look over your list. Make any changes you like and briefly note why the changes were made.

About 150 million years ago, reptiles dominated the Earth.

4–1 Reptiles

On the barren, windswept shoreline of the Galapagos Islands in the Pacific Ocean, a group of large lizards called marine iguanas (ih-GWAH-nuhz) cling to the rocks. Wave after wave splash against the rocks, but the iguanas do not let go. Suddenly, the iguanas plunge into the cold sea. Their lashing tails and webbed feet propel them through the water as they dive for the seaweed on which they feed. With their bodies chilled by the water, the iguanas soon scramble back onto the rocks to warm up.

Iguanas are just one example of the group of vertebrates known as reptiles. Other reptiles include snakes, turtles, crocodiles, and extinct (no longer living) animals such as dinosaurs and pterodactyls.

Reptiles are vertebrates that have lungs, scaly skin, and a special type of egg. These characteristics, which you will soon read about in more detail, make it possible for reptiles to spend their entire lives out of water. Another important characteristic

Figure 4–1 *The four living scientific groups of reptiles are represented by the spectacled caiman (top left), Florida red-bellied turtle (top right), tuatara (bottom left), and marine iguana (bottom right).*

Figure 4–2 *The earliest known reptiles resembled a cross between a lizard and a toad. What characteristics make reptiles better suited than amphibians for life on land?*

of living reptiles involves the way they control their body temperature. **All living reptiles are cold-blooded.** Do you recall from Chapter 3 how cold-blooded animals control their body temperature?

Reptiles appeared hundreds of millions of years ago, soon after the first amphibians. As you can see in Figure 4–2, the first reptiles were large, fat, short-legged animals that resembled a cross between a lizard and a toad. Although the first reptiles looked a lot like the ancient amphibians that dominated the Earth at that time, there were several important differences. These differences enabled early reptiles and their descendants (modern reptiles, birds, and mammals) to inhabit all sorts of land environments. As you read about the characteristics of modern reptiles, focus on the ways in which these characteristics make reptiles better suited to life on land than amphibians.

Reptiles have skins that are completely covered by a tough, dry, relatively thick layer of scales. These scales are formed by the outermost layer of the skin. They are made of dead, flattened cells that contain the same hard, tough substance found in your fingernails. The scales form an unbroken waterproof covering that helps to prevent drying out.

Although the waterproof skin helps to prevent excess water loss, it also makes it impossible for a typical reptile to breathe through its skin. A thin, moist membrane is needed to transport oxygen from the environment into the body and carbon dioxide from the body to the environment. Because a typical reptile (unlike a typical amphibian) does not have skin that is thin and moist, it depends entirely on its lungs for gas exchange. Would you expect the lungs of reptiles to be more complex or less complex than those of amphibians? Why?

The waterproof scaly skin is not the only reptilian adaptation for preventing excess water loss. The kidneys of reptiles concentrate nitrogen-containing waste products so that as little water as possible is lost when wastes are eliminated.

ACTIVITY READING

It All Depends on Your Point of View

We humans tend to believe that being warm-blooded, live-bearing, and mammalian are the best things to be. But suppose that an intelligent cold-blooded reptilian life form had evolved. Would it have viewed things the same way?

For one writer's view of a reptile-dominated Earth, read the novel *West of Eden* by Harry Harrison.

Figure 4–3 *As new skin grows in, land vertebrates shed bits of the old, dead, outermost layers of skin. Reptiles such as the chameleon shed their old skin all at once (left). The outermost layer of skin forms a chameleon's horns (center), a rattlesnake's rattle (right), and other structures.*

ACTIVITY

DISCOVERING

Eggs-amination

1. Obtain a fresh chicken egg. Examine it with a magnifying glass.

2. Gently crack the egg into a bowl.

3. Examine the inside of the shell. Look at the blunt end of the egg. What do you find there? Fill one half of the eggshell with water. What do you observe?

4. Examine the contents of the egg. What are the functions of the different parts? What part is the egg cell?

5. Look for a small white spot on the yolk. This marks the spot where the embryo would have developed if the egg had been fertilized.

■ How does the structure of the egg and its shell help it to perform its functions?

Reptiles, like adult amphibians, have a double-loop circulatory system. In some reptiles—crocodiles and their relatives, to be exact—the two loops are completely separate. The oxygen-poor blood in one loop never mixes with the oxygen-rich blood in the other loop. Because the bloods never mix, oxygen is delivered more efficiently to the cells of the body. How does this double-loop system differ from the double-loop system in amphibians?

Reptiles have a brain and nervous system quite similar to that of an amphibian, although the brain may be slightly better developed. Most reptile sense organs are well developed, although there are some exceptions. For example, snakes are deaf, and certain burrowing lizards lack eyes.

The scaly skin, improved breathing system, and water-conserving method of waste elimination helped to make early reptiles better suited for life on land than the amphibians that had come before them. But perhaps the reptiles' most important adaptation for living on land was their special egg.

The eggs of fishes and amphibians are delicate sacs that contain stored food and a developing organism. These eggs dry out easily and thus require a watery or extremely damp environment in which to develop. In contrast, the eggs of reptiles can be laid under forest logs, in beach sand, or in cracks in desert rocks. Why is this so?

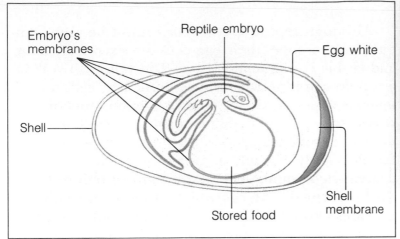

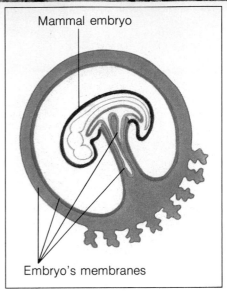

Figure 4–4 *These hognose snakes seem to be pleased by their first glimpse of the world. The membranes that surround reptiles as they develop within the egg are shown in the diagram on the left. These membranes also surround developing mammals, as shown in the diagram on the right.*

Figure 4–4 shows the structures that make it possible for the embryos in reptile eggs to develop on dry land. As you can see, the egg is surrounded by a protective shell that prevents the contents of the egg from drying out. Most reptile eggs have a shell that is tough but a bit flexible—sort of like leather. A few reptile eggs have a hard shell similar to the one on a chicken egg. Although the shell looks solid, it is actually dotted with tiny holes large enough for gases to move in and out but small enough to prevent water from easily escaping. Within the shell are several membranes and a watery fluid, which along with the shell provide further protection for the developing embryo.

The reptilian egg is of great evolutionary importance for two reasons. First, it freed vertebrates from their dependence on water for reproduction and development. Second, it clearly links reptiles to the vertebrates that evolved from them: birds and mammals. Bird eggs have the same basic structure as reptile eggs. And the same membranes that protect and support a reptile or a bird embryo also protect and support mammal embryos.

Fertilization in reptiles is internal. Recall that internal fertilization means that a sperm cell joins with an egg cell inside the parent's body. Why is it necessary for animals with tough, waterproof shells on their eggs to have internal fertilization?

Figure 4–5 *Young reptiles, such as the baby box turtle and newly born copperheads, look like miniature versions of their parents. How does this pattern of development differ from that in most amphibians?*

ACTIVITY

DOING

Snakes

Visit a pet store that sells snakes. Observe the various types of snakes that are for sale. Interview the pet shop owner or one of the workers. Find out the feeding habits of each snake and how to care for one at home. Present your findings to the class in an oral report accompanied by a poster showing your observations.

Although reptile sperm cells cannot be seen without a microscope, their egg cells are extremely large and visible to the unaided eye. The yellowish yolk in a reptile egg is actually the egg cell. Egg cells are immense because they contain huge amounts of stored food. After an egg is fertilized, the female's body builds a shell around it. In some reptiles, the female's body may add a layer of egg white (a thick protein-rich liquid) around the egg cell before the shell is formed. The egg white cushions the embryo, provides extra protein and water, and helps to prevent bacterial infections.

Most reptiles lay their eggs soon after the shells have formed. However, a few reptiles, such as certain snakes and lizards, protect their eggs by retaining them inside the body for part or all of the time it takes for the embryo to reach the stage at which it is ready to be hatched. In almost all reptiles in which the offspring are born alive, the developing young are nourished entirely by the yolk. In a small minority of live bearers, a special connection develops between the embryo's outermost membrane and the body of the female. Through this connection, food and oxygen are delivered from the female's body to her developing offspring. Reptile embryos with this special connection typically have much less yolk than embryos without this connection. Why do you think this is so?

Whether they hatch from eggs or are born alive, young reptiles look like miniature adults. Unlike most amphibians, reptiles do not undergo metamorphosis. Because reptile eggs develop and hatch on land, there is no need for young reptiles to go through an immature water-dwelling stage. They can complete their development inside the safety of the eggshell. How does the more complete development of a reptile relate to the fact that reptile eggs contain a larger amount of yolk than typical amphibian eggs do?

Lizards and Snakes

"Here be dragons" ancient maps sometimes declared about the faraway, poorly known lands at their edges. Of course, as travel to distant places increased, it soon became apparent that there were

no fire-breathing winged reptilian monsters any-where in the world.

But as things turned out, there are dragons—of a sort. In the early part of this century—so the story goes—a pioneering pilot was trying to fly a plane from the islands of Indonesia to Australia. About 1500 kilometers east of Djakarta, the capital of Indonesia, the pilot developed engine trouble and was forced to land on a tiny volcanic island called Komodo. While the pilot tried to repair the engine, the dragons appeared and charged toward him.

The dragons were giant reptiles about 3 meters long and 160 kilograms in mass. They had scaly brownish hides, clawed feet, powerful tails, and short strong legs. Their long, forked tongues flickered in and out of their mouths like thin orange flames. The pilot probably did not wait to see the dragons' teeth before retreating to the safety of the cockpit.

Fortunately, the pilot was able to repair his engine. Although the dragons of Komodo usually hunt animals such as chickens, goats, small deer, and pigs, they are capable of killing large animals such as water buffaloes and humans.

The pilot's tale, along with similar stories from Indonesian pearl divers and fishers, prompted an expedition to obtain scientific specimens of the drag-ons. In 1912, the Komodo dragon was given its sci-entific name and correctly identified as a lizard—the largest (in terms of both length and mass) species of lizard in existence today.

Lizards are reptiles that typically have slender bodies, movable eyelids, long tails, four legs, and

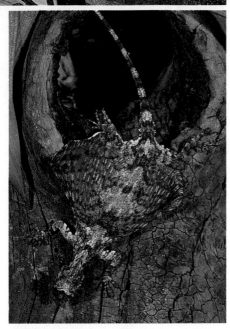

Figure 4–6 *Fire-breathing they are not, but all these lizards are known as dragons. The Komodo dragon (top left), water dragon (top right), and flying dragon (bottom) make their home in Southeast Asia. When fully spread, the reddish flaps of skin and ribs on the flying dragon's sides form "wings," which allow it to glide from tree to tree.*

Figure 4–7 *A basilisk can run across the surface of small ponds and streams (bottom right). Geckos have suction-cuplike toes that enable them to walk up vertical panes of glass and run upside down across ceilings (top right). The horned lizard, which is often called a "horned toad," changes color. This helps it to blend in with its surroundings and to better absorb or reflect heat (left).*

clawed toes. They are placed in the same group of reptiles as snakes. Lizards range in size from tiny geckos 3 centimeters long to tree-dwelling monitor lizards of New Guinea that are more than 4.5 meters long. And as you can see in Figure 4–7, the shapes of lizards also vary.

For the most part, lizards are insect eaters that capture their prey by waiting for it to come nearby. When the prey is within range, the lizard lunges forward and grabs its meal in its jaws. Some lizards have evolved interesting variations on this maneuver. Slow-moving chameleons flick their long sticky tongue out of their mouth and then snap it back inside with a meal attached. The Gila (HEE-lah) monster of the American Southwest subdues its prey by poisoning it. After the Gila monster bites its prey, it hangs onto it tightly. A slow-acting poison made by glands in the lizard's lower jaw flows along grooves in the teeth and into the wounded prey. Contrary to popular stories, Gila monsters do not attack humans unless severely provoked. And although Gila monster bites are not deadly, they are extremely painful.

Figure 4–8 *Zap! A chameleon nabs its dinner with a flick of its long sticky tongue. How does the Gila monster catch and subdue its prey?*

Some lizards have special adaptations that help them to avoid becoming another animal's dinner. Chameleons are one of several kinds of lizards that can change color to match their surroundings. Other lizards have an even stranger way of protecting themselves. If threatened or captured by a predator, these lizards shed their tail. The castoff tail thrashes on the ground, confusing the predator and giving the lizard a chance to escape. Later the lizard grows back the missing tail.

Snakes are basically lizards that have lost their limbs, eyelids, and ears during the course of their evolution into burrowing forms more than 80 million years ago. Surprisingly, these losses did not restrict snakes to being burrowers forever. Snakes are an evolutionary success story—there are many species that live in many different kinds of habitats throughout the world.

A snake moves by wriggling its long, thin, muscular body. The scales on its belly help the animal to grip the surface on which it is moving and push itself forward. Special kinds of wriggling motions enable desert snakes to move across loose desert sand and allow tree-dwelling snakes to creep silently along branches. Many snakes are at home in the water and can swim at the surface or remain submerged. Sea snakes, which spend their entire lives in the ocean, have flattened, paddle-shaped tails that help them to swim swiftly.

Contrary to expressions such as "slimy as a snake," snakes are not at all slimy. They are actually rather pleasant to the touch—cool, dry, and smooth,

Figure 4–9 *In some lizards, the tail is structured in such a way that it can break off cleanly. Look closely and you can see the lizard's lost tail in the foreground. How do breakaway tails help lizards to survive?*

Figure 4–10 *Many snakes, such as the sea snake (top left) and the Siamese cobra (bottom left), have attractive colors and markings. The blue snake is a rare form of the green tree python (right).*

with little grooves around the edges of the scales. A word of warning, however: Snakes should be handled only under the supervision of an expert. Even tame nonpoisonous snakes can inflict painful bites.

Because snakes feed on small animals such as rats and mice, they can be quite helpful to people. But because some snakes are poisonous, people often try to get rid of all the snakes in an area. How would such an action affect the rat and mouse population in that area?

Snakes have a number of interesting adaptations for obtaining food. Although snakes are deaf and have poor eyesight, their other senses make up for these limitations. When a snake flicks its tongue in and out of its mouth, it is actually bringing particles in the air to a special sense organ on the roof of its mouth. This organ "analyzes" chemicals in the air, enabling the snake to find food. Many snakes are able to detect the body heat produced by their prey through special pits on the sides of their head.

Some snakes have glands in their upper jaw that produce a poison that immobilizes their prey. This poison is injected into the prey through special teeth called fangs. Four kinds of poisonous snakes make their home in the United States: rattlesnakes, copperheads, water moccasins, and coral snakes. Other poisonous snakes—such as the king cobra, which is the largest poisonous snake in the world—live on other continents.

Turtles

Turtles are reptiles whose bodies are enclosed in a shell. The shell of a turtle consists of plates of bone covered by shields made of the same substance as scales. Some turtles have extremely strong shells that can support a weight 200 times greater than their own. This is roughly equivalent to your being able to hold two elephants on your back! Not all turtles have hard, bony shells. The leatherback sea turtle, the largest living turtle, has only a few small pieces of bone embedded in the skin of its back.

Turtles do not have teeth. Instead, they have beaks that are similar in structure to the beaks of birds. Many turtles eat plants as well as animals. The alligator snapping turtle has a particularly interesting adaptation for obtaining food. The turtle lies absolutely still on the bottom of a river or pond, looking like a rock or log. The only part of the turtle that moves is a small wormlike structure on the floor of its mouth. When a hungry fish swims into the turtle's mouth to eat the wriggling ''worm,'' the turtle snaps its jaws closed and swallows the fish.

Figure 4–11 *Imagine trying to swallow something as big as your head! This action is impossible for humans, but snakes do it all the time. How do the tongue, teeth, and body muscles of snakes help them to obtain food?*

Figure 4–12 *Land-dwelling turtles with domed shells are often called tortoises (top left). The leatherback, the largest living species of turtle, leaves the ocean only to lay its eggs (top right). The desert tortoise uses its beak to nip off tasty bits of plants (bottom left). The matamata of South America spends most of its time hiding among the dead leaves and mud at the bottom of streams (bottom right). It feeds by sucking in water and unwary fishes like a vacuum cleaner.*

Sea turtles known as green turtles are among the most outstanding navigators in the animal kingdom. Soon after hatching, the young turtles head for the ocean. There they wander for many years over thousands of square kilometers. Eventually, the turtles mature and mate. Ready to lay their own eggs, these turtles do something quite amazing. They return to the same beach where they were born!

That beach may be hundreds of kilometers away, across an ocean surface that has no road signs or other markings. Yet the turtles find their way home. How? Recently, scientists have discovered that sea turtles are able to use wave motion and magnetic fields to maintain their direction.

Figure 4–13 *Sea turtles spend most of their lives at sea. But when they are ready to lay their eggs, the turtles return to the same beaches where they were hatched.*

Alligators and Crocodiles

Alligators and crocodiles are large meat-eating lizardlike reptiles that spend much of their time in water. They have long snouts, powerful tails, and thick, armored skin. Although alligators and crocodiles are similar, it is not difficult to tell them apart. Alligators have broad, rounded snouts, whereas crocodiles have narrow, pointed snouts. When an alligator's mouth is closed, only a few of the teeth on its lower jaw are visible. When a crocodile's mouth is closed, most of its teeth are visible. But don't be taken in by the crocodile's welcoming grin. Crocodiles are far more aggressive than alligators, and some species are known to eat humans!

When they are not lying on riverbanks basking in the sun or resting in the shade, alligators and crocodiles spend their time submerged in water. Although these reptiles look lazy and slow, they are capable of moving rapidly, both in water and on land.

Alligators and crocodiles do most of their hunting at night. They eat everything from insects, fishes, and amphibians to birds and large hoofed mammals. (Larger alligators and crocodiles typically hunt larger prey.)

Alligators and crocodiles build nests of mud or plants in which they lay their hard-shelled eggs. In some species, the eggs are abandoned after they are laid. But in other species, the female takes good care of her eggs and offspring.

Figure 4–14 *After her eggs hatch, a female alligator or crocodile will carry her babies in her jaws. The female will continue to care for her young—often with the help of the male.*

Figure 4–15 *Alligators have broad, rounded snouts (bottom left). Crocodiles have narrow, pointed snouts and a distinctive toothy "grin" (bottom right). The gharial of India belongs to the same group of reptiles as alligators and crocodiles (top).*

PROBLEM Solving

Alligator Anxieties

The purely imaginary Gatorville Amateur Conservationist Society (GACS) is faced with a puzzling situation. Three months ago, the Gatorville swamp was drained to make way for a new shopping mall. The adult alligators in the swamp were moved to a wildlife refuge elsewhere in the state. GACS volunteers rescued the newly laid eggs from the alligator nests and placed them in specially designed incubators.

The temperature of all the incubators was set at 30°C. One incubator, however, had a faulty thermostat. The actual temperature in this incubator was 4°C higher than what was indicated on the dials. This problem was not discovered until the eggs had been in the incubators for three weeks.

To everyone's delight, most of the rescued alligator eggs did hatch. But an examination of the baby alligators revealed something strange: All of the

babies from the normal incubators were females, and all the babies from the faulty incubator were males. Why?

Designing an Experiment

1. Develop a hypothesis to explain the results of the alligator-hatching project.

2. Design an experiment to test your hypothesis. What do you expect the results of your experiment to be?

3. If your hypothesis proves to be correct, how might this information affect future conservation efforts?

4–1 Section Review

1. Describe three ways in which reptiles are adapted for life on land.
2. How does the structure of the egg help it to perform its function?
3. Compare the three major groups of reptiles.

Connection—*Wildlife Conservation*
4. Conservationists are concerned, that once sea turtles that nest on a particular beach are killed off, there will never be sea turtles on that beach again. Explain why.

4–2 Birds

People's admiration and affection for birds are reflected in the frequent use of birds as symbols. The eagle shows up on the back of quarters and on postage stamps as the national emblem of the United States. Certain airlines and other businesses feature birds in their emblems. Even sports teams are named after birds. The Toronto Blue Jays, Seattle Seahawks, and Phoenix Cardinals are just three such teams. Can you name others?

Many people think that birds are the most fascinating and colorful animals on Earth. One reason for this is that birds can fly. Along with bats and insects, birds are the only animals with the power of flight, although not all species of birds fly.

Birds are relatively recent additions to the parade of life. Because the skeletons of many small dinosaurs are almost identical to the skeletons of the earliest birds, there is much controversy over which fossils are those of birds and when birds first appeared on Earth. The oldest fossil that is definitely that of a bird is of *Archaeopteryx* (ahr-kee-AHP-ter-ihks). The root word *archaeo-* means ancient, and the root word *-pteryx* means wing. Why is *Archaeopteryx* an appropriate name?

Archaeopteryx lived about 140 million years ago, during a time when dinosaurs and other reptiles ruled the Earth. As you can see in Figure 4–16, this bird did not look much like modern birds. It had a long bony tail and sharp teeth, neither of which is found in modern birds. It had clawed fingers and many other odd features not typical of birds. Despite all the ways in which it was different from modern birds, *Archaeopteryx* was definitely a bird. For around its fossilized bones are the unmistakable impressions of feathers.

Birds are warmblooded egg-laying vertebrates that have feathers. All modern birds—including ostriches, penguins, and other flightless birds—evolved from ancestors that could fly. As you read about birds, focus on the ways in which their characteristics reflect their heritage of flight.

The single most important characteristic of birds is **feathers.** Feathers, like the scales of reptiles, are

Figure 4–16 *The fossilized remains of* Archaeopteryx *show the shadowy outlines of the feathers that covered the wings and tail. An artist's reconstruction shows how this ancient bird may have appeared when it was alive.*

Figure 4–17 *Body feathers help to insulate the mourning dove, and feathers on its wings and tail help it to fly (left). The brightly colored feathers of the rainbow lorikeets help them to communicate (right). Feathers also hide birds from predators. Can you locate the four ptarmigans (center)?*

ctivity Bank

Do Oil and Water Mix?, p.163

ACTIVITY

DISCOVERING

Comparing Feathers

Obtain a few samples of feathers. Try to obtain both down and contour feathers. How are the feathers similar? How are they different?

Gently run your fingers along a contour feather from its tip to its base. What happens? What happens if you rub the feather in the opposite direction?

■ How are feathers put together?

■ How does the structure of a feather help it to perform its functions?

made of dead cells that contain the same material found in your fingernails. Feathers come in many colors, shapes, and sizes. Body feathers help to insulate the body. Feathers on the wings and tail are used in flying. Dull-colored, speckled feathers may help a bird to blend in with its background, hiding it from its natural enemies. Brightly colored feathers help a bird to communicate with other members of its species. For example, the brilliant feathers of male birds such as peacocks advertise their presence to potential mates.

The feathers on the wings and on most of a bird's body are called **contour feathers.** Contour feathers are the largest and most familiar feathers. They give birds their streamlined shape. Other feathers—called **down**—are short, fluffy feathers that act as insulation. Most birds have down feathers on their breasts. As you can see in Figure 4–18, baby birds are often covered with down. As the baby birds grow up, contour feathers grow in and most of the down falls out. Why do you think down from birds such as geese is often used in coats and quilts?

Have you ever heard the expression "eats like a bird"? This phrase, which is used to describe someone who eats very little, was certainly not invented by someone familiar with birds. For birds "eat like pigs." In fact, birds are even bigger eaters than pigs. Because they are warmblooded, birds must expend energy in order to maintain their body temperature. Flying also demands great amounts of energy. In order to meet these energy demands, birds must acquire a lot of energy in the form of food. A pigeon eats about 6.5 percent of its body weight in seeds, crumbs, and other foods every day. A hummingbird eats about twice its weight in nectar (a sugary liquid produced by flowers) daily. How much food would you have to eat every day if you ate like a pigeon? If you ate like a hummingbird?

Birds eat many different kinds of foods, including microscopic blue-green bacteria, fruits and seeds, insects, other birds, mice, monkeys, and the remains of dead animals. The beak of a bird is often remarkably adapted for the type of food it eats. Hawks and owls have sharp, curved beaks used for tearing their prey into pieces small enough to be swallowed. Kiwis and woodcocks have long, thin beaks that are used to probe into the soil for earthworms. Cardinals and sparrows have thick blunt beaks with which they crush the hard shells of seeds.

Bird adaptations for flight are not limited to the outside of the body. Bird bones are hollow and

Figure 4–18 *Birds have fluffy down feathers and leaf-shaped contour feathers. As this young frigate bird grows older, most of its whitish baby down will be replaced by glossy black adult feathers.*

Figure 4–19 *You might think that a toucan's enormous beak would cause the bird to tip over. But the beak is hollow and light for its size (top left). The puffin's tall, flat beak serves as a shovel for digging nesting holes. It is also a handy fish holder (top right). The pelican's pouched beak scoops fishes from the water like a net (bottom).*

Figure 4–20 *Some birds store food. A shrike kills prey and then hangs them on thorns and twigs. This shrike looks quite pleased about the striped caterpillar it has caught. How does an acorn woodpecker store food?*

Activity Bank

An Eggs-aggeration, p.164

therefore quite lightweight. Like the bones, the internal organs of birds have evolved in ways that enable birds to fly efficiently. The respiratory system is more advanced in birds than in any other class of vertebrates. How does this relate to the energy needs of birds? (*Hint:* Oxygen is needed to break down food to obtain energy.)

Birds have special structures called air sacs attached to their lungs. The air sacs inflate and deflate in a complex way to ensure that a supply of fresh air is constantly moving in one direction through the lungs. The great efficiency with which birds perform the function of gas exchange is particularly apparent at high altitudes, where the air is thin. Mountain climbers on Mount Everest must carry tanks of oxygen and stop often to rest. Their lungs cannot obtain oxygen efficiently enough to permit long periods of strenuous activity. As the mountain climbers rest, they may observe Himalayan geese flying overhead. The lungs of geese can obtain oxygen efficiently enough to permit the extremely strenuous task of flying. The geese even have spare air—which they use to honk a greeting as they soar past the out-of-breath mountain climbers!

Birds have a double-loop circulatory system in which the two loops are completely separated. This helps to ensure that the oxygen provided by the lungs is delivered effectively to the cells of the body.

Like reptiles and amphibians, birds have two long, oval kidneys that filter nitrogen-containing wastes from the blood. Birds produce the same kind of concentrated nitrogen-containing waste product as land-dwelling reptiles.

Although the term "bird-brained" means stupid, birds are actually quite intelligent. Like the rest of their nervous system, their brain is well developed. The eyesight of many birds—hawks, vultures, and eagles, to name a few—is far keener than that of humans. Some birds have an extraordinarily sharp sense of hearing. The faintest rustle of a mouse as it creeps across the forest floor is all that a hunting owl needs to pinpoint the location of its next meal.

The reproductive organs in birds are often tiny and compact. Only during the breeding season do these organs enlarge to a functional size. All female birds lay eggs. No birds, past or present, bear their young alive. How do these two characteristics of bird reproduction affect flying ability?

Bird eggs, which have the same basic structure as reptile eggs, contain a generous supply of egg white and are covered by a hard shell. Because bird eggs will develop only if they are kept at the proper temperature, almost all are cared for by the parent birds. In some species, only one parent cares for the eggs. In other species, both parents take turns keeping the eggs warm.

In almost all birds, the parents' duties are not finished when the eggs hatch. In some birds, such as chickens and ducks, the young have feathers when they hatch, and they are soon able to run about and feed themselves. However, they still depend on their parents for protection. In other birds, the young are featherless, blind, and helpless when they hatch. Their parents must feed and care for them until they are old enough to fly and take care of themselves.

Bird Behavior

Have you ever heard a bird singing cheerfully on a fine spring day? If you have, you might have wondered what all the excitement was about. Perhaps you might have thought that the bird was happy.

Figure 4–21 Most birds, such as the skimmer, crouch over their eggs to keep them warm (bottom). An Adelie penguin keeps its egg warm by balancing it on its feet (top).

Figure 4–22 Some birds are well-developed when they hatch. The newly hatched Canada geese will soon be waddling through the grass and swimming in the water—with a little encouragement from their parent! Others are featherless, blind, and helpless when they hatch. These newly hatched pelicans will be completely dependent on their parents for quite some time.

Activity Bank

Strictly for the Birds, p.165

Figure 4–23 *Male birds have many ways of attracting a mate. A peacock spreads the long, colorful plumes of his tail and struts about. The male frigate bird puffs up his bright red throat sac. Male weaverbirds demonstrate their skills at nest-building.*

Figure 4–24 *The meadowlark has one of the loveliest songs in nature. Why do birds sing?*

Birds actually sing for rather serious reasons. Early in the breeding season, birds sing to attract a mate and to warn other birds of the same sex to stay away. The song establishes or maintains a **territory.** A territory is an area where an individual bird (or any other animal) lives. Establishing a territory is important because it ensures that fewer birds will compete for food and living space in the same area. Birds may also sing to warn of danger, to threaten an enemy, or to communicate other sorts of information.

Birds communicate with signals that are seen as well as with signals that are heard. The bright feathers of some male birds are used to attract females and to scare off rivals. However, brightly colored feathers also make the bird more noticeable to predators. Can you explain why many birds sport bright colors only during the breeding season?

Some birds attract a mate by doing something unusual. Male bowerbirds build large and colorful constructions of twigs to make females notice them. They may even paint their bowers with berry juice or decorate them with feathers, shells, butterfly wings, and flowers. Male weaverbirds construct a nest that is examined by a prospective mate for soundness and craftsmanship. A male penguin does not construct anything. Instead, he presents his intended mate with a pebble. The pebble indicates that he is ready to breed and to care for a youngster.

Most birds build nests, which are designed to protect the eggs and the young birds as they develop. These nests can be little more than a shallow trench hollowed out in the ground or they can be quite elaborate. Hummingbird nests are tiny cups woven out of spider silk, decorated with bits of plants, and lined with feathers.

Many birds **migrate,** or move to a new environment during the course of a year. Some birds migrate over tremendous distances. For example, the American golden plover flies more than 25,000 kilometers when it migrates. Birds migrate for many reasons, but probably the most important reason is to follow seasonal food supplies. Birds have developed extremely accurate mechanisms for migrating. Scientists have learned that some birds navigate by observing the sun and other stars. Other birds follow coastlines or mountain ranges. Still other birds are believed to have magnetic centers in their brains. These centers act as a compass does to help the bird find its way.

ACTIVITY READING

Rara Aves

This Latin phrase, which literally means rare birds, is used to refer to any type of extraordinary thing. There are a number of works of literature that feature birds in their titles.

A few of these *rara aves* are *The Trumpet of the Swan* by E. B. White; *Jonathan Livingston Seagull* by Richard Bach; *To Kill a Mockingbird* by Harper Lee, and *I Know Why the Caged Bird Sings* by Maya Angelou.

Figure 4–25 *The nests of barn swallows are round clay pots built one beakful of mud at a time. The nests of certain African weaverbirds have several "rooms." The nest mounds built by mallee fowl are up to 4.5 meters high and 10 meters across.*

Types of Birds

There are about 8700 living species of birds. These species are divided among roughly 30 scientific classification groups. As you might imagine, such diversity among birds makes it impossible to discuss all the scientific groups in detail. To simplify matters, birds are often divided into a few broad categories according to one or two significant characteristics. Although these nonscientific categories give no information about evolutionary relationships and also exclude a number of birds, they do provide a glimpse of the enormous diversity among birds.

Most familiar birds are commonly known as songbirds. Cardinals, sparrows, and robins are examples of songbirds. Songbirds range in size from tiny flycatchers 8 centimeters long to birds of paradise whose elegant tail feathers make them more than a meter long. Songbirds have feet that are well adapted for perching on branches, electric wires, and other narrow horizontal structures.

As their name indicates, many songbirds sing beautifully. Nightingales, mockingbirds, warblers, and canaries make some of the loveliest sounds in the natural world. However, some birds with ugly voices—crows and ravens, for example—are also

Figure 4–26 *Songbirds, more correctly known as perching birds, include the scarlet-chested sunbird of Africa (top), the robin of Europe (bottom left), and the Gouldian finch of Australia (bottom right).*

placed in this group. Thus songbirds are more appropriately known as perching birds.

Hunting birds such as hawks, eagles, and owls are known as birds of prey. Birds of prey are superb fliers with keen eyesight. Soaring high in the air, they can spot prey on the ground or in the water far below them. Birds of prey eat fishes, reptiles, mammals, and other birds. Some even eat small monkeys.

Birds of prey are able to fly very fast. The peregrine falcon has been clocked at more than 125 kilometers per hour while diving at its prey. Birds of prey have sharp claws, called talons, on their toes. Talons enable the bird to grasp its prey. Some eagles have talons that are longer than the fangs of a lion. Birds of prey also have strong, curved beaks that are used to tear their prey into pieces small enough to be swallowed.

The birds that swim and dive in lakes and ponds are known as waterfowl. Swans and ducks are typical waterfowl. These birds glide across the surface of the water, propelled by webbed feet that resemble paddles. Occasionally, they duck their head and neck into the water to nibble at water plants with their broad, flat beak.

During the course of evolution, some birds have lost their ability to fly. The wings of these birds are

Figure 4–27 *The king vulture of South America (bottom left), the monkey-eating eagle of the Philippines (bottom right), and the bald eagle of North America (top) are examples of birds of prey.*

Figure 4–28 *Swans (left) and geese (right) are types of waterfowl. What are the main characteristics of waterfowl?*

small compared to the size of their body. Some flightless birds are specialized as runners. Such birds include the ostrich of Africa (the largest bird alive today), the rhea of South America, and the emu and cassowary of Australia. These birds have strong leg muscles that enable them to run quickly and to defend themselves against any enemy foolish enough to challenge them. Penguins are flightless birds that are specialized as swimmers. On land, penguins waddle and hop awkwardly. But in water, they are swift and graceful.

Figure 4–29 *The cassowary of New Guinea (top) and the ostrich of Africa (bottom right) have long, powerful legs that enable them to run swiftly. The comical parade of king penguins shows that penguins cannot move quickly on land (bottom left). However, penguins are remarkably swift swimmers. To what nonscientific category do these three types of birds belong?*

CONNECTIONS

Flights of Fancy

When people talk about the beauty of birds, they usually focus on the spectacular colors of the feathers or the lovely melody of the songs. But it is clear that the beauty of the movement of birds has not been lost on the dancers of the world.

For thousands of years, humans have tried to capture the grace and power of birds in *dance.* The mating dance of the crane—with its spectacular leaps, bows, and flapping of wings—is echoed in some of the dances of the Australian aborigines. The majestic, soaring flight of the eagle is re-created in special Native American ceremonial dances. And the graceful, gliding movement of swans while swimming and while in flight is imitated in ballets such as *Swan Lake.*

4–2 Section Review

1. Describe the major characteristics of birds. Which characteristics are adaptations for flight?
2. What is the difference between down and contour feathers? How are feathers adapted to different functions?
3. How are birds similar to reptiles? How are they different?
4. Name and briefly describe four nonscientific categories of birds.

Critical Thinking—*Making Inferences*
5. The kiwi is a chicken-sized bird that is covered with long brownish hairlike feathers and has no visible wings. It has a very long beak, rather short legs, and feet similar to a chicken's. What do you think this bird eats? What can you infer about the kiwi's behavior, environment, and evolution?

ACTIVITY THINKING

A Flock of Phrases

Have you ever been accused of being bird-brained? What other common phrases can you think of that have to do with birds? Get together with a friend or two and see how many you can identify. Based on what you know about birds, determine whether they are accurate.

Laboratory Investigation

Owl Pellets

Problem

What does an owl eat?

Materials

owl pellet	magnifying glass
dissecting needle	small metric ruler

Procedure 🧪 🗄

1. Observe the outside of an owl pellet and record your observations.
2. Gently break the pellet into two pieces.
3. Using the dissecting needle, separate any undigested bones and fur from the pellet. Remove all fur from any skulls in the pellet.
4. Group similar bones together in a pile. For example, put all skulls in one group. Observe the skulls. Record the length, number, shape, and color of the teeth.
5. Now try to fit together bones from the different piles to form skeletons.

Observations

1. What does an owl pellet look like? What is it made of?
2. What kinds of bones were the most numerous?
3. What kinds of bones seem to have been missing from the prey?

Analysis and Conclusions

1. What animals were eaten by the owl?
2. Which animals appear to be eaten most frequently by the owl?
3. Why do you think owls cough up pellets?
4. What can you infer about the owl's characteristics from the animals it eats?
5. **On Your Own**   Design a study that uses owl pellets to answer a question about the feeding habits of owls. For example, your study might determine whether owls feed on different kinds of prey during different parts of the year.

Shrew	Upper jaw has at least 18 teeth. Skull length is 23 mm or less. Teeth are brown.	
House mouse	Upper jaw has 2 biting teeth. Upper jaw extends past lower jaw. Skull length is 22 mm or less.	
Meadow vole	Upper jaw has 2 biting teeth. Upper jaw does not extend past lower jaw. Molar teeth are flat.	
Mole	Upper jaw has at least 18 teeth. Skull length is 23 mm or more.	
Rat	Upper jaw has 2 biting teeth. Upper jaw extends past lower jaw. Skull length is 22 mm or more.	

Summarizing Key Concepts

4–1 Reptiles

▲ Reptiles are vertebrates that have lungs, scaly skin, and a special type of egg.

▲ All living reptiles are coldblooded.

▲ Reptiles have a number of adaptations that make them well suited for life on land.

▲ Reptiles have a double-loop circulatory system. In most reptiles, the two loops are not completely separated.

▲ Land-dwelling reptiles excrete a concentrated nitrogen-containing waste, which helps them to conserve water.

▲ Reptiles have internal fertilization.

▲ A typical reptile egg has a shell and several membranes that protect the developing embryo.

▲ Most reptiles lay eggs; a few reptiles bear live young.

▲ Some reptiles care for their eggs and young.

▲ One scientific group of reptiles includes lizards and snakes.

▲ One scientific group of reptiles is composed of turtles, which are reptiles whose bodies are enclosed by a two-part shell.

▲ One scientific group of reptiles includes crocodiles and alligators.

4–2 Birds

▲ Birds are warmblooded, egg-laying vertebrates that have feathers.

▲ The bodies of birds are adapted for flight. However, not all species of birds can fly.

▲ Feathers, such as contour feathers and down, have shapes that help them to perform their functions.

▲ Bird beaks and feet show a number of interesting adaptations.

▲ The respiratory system is more advanced in birds than in any other vertebrates. The bird's air sacs enable air to be constantly moved through the lungs in one direction.

▲ Birds have a double-loop circulatory system in which the loops are completely separated.

▲ Almost all birds care for their eggs and young.

▲ Birds have many complex behaviors.

▲ One reason birds sing is to establish and maintain a territory.

▲ Many birds migrate.

▲ Four nonscientific—but useful—categories of birds are songbirds, birds of prey, waterfowl, and flightless birds.

Reviewing Key Terms

Define each term in a complete sentence.

4–2 Birds
feather
contour feather
down
territory
migrate

Chapter Review

Content Review

Multiple Choice

Choose the letter of the answer that best completes each statement.

1. Which of these is a bird of prey?
   a. eagle
   b. pigeon
   c. toucan
   d. ostrich
2. All living reptiles
   a. lay eggs.
   b. spend their entire lives on land.
   c. undergo metamorphosis.
   d. have lungs.
3. The characteristic that separates birds from all other vertebrates is their
   a. claws.
   b. feathers.
   c. egg-laying.
   d. flight.
4. Down feathers
   a. are shaped like leaves.
   b. include large flight feathers on wings.
   c. act as insulation.
   d. all of these

5. Birds sing to
   a. establish a territory.
   b. attract a mate.
   c. warn of danger.
   d. all of these
6. A four-legged water-dwelling shelled reptile that lays leathery-shelled eggs is classified as a(an)
   a. alligator.
   b. crocodile.
   c. turtle.
   d. lizard.
7. To follow seasonal food supplies, birds
   a. perch.
   b. migrate.
   c. build a nest.
   d. hibernate.
8. All reptile eggs
   a. must be laid in water.
   b. have a leathery shell.
   c. are fertilized externally.
   d. contain protective membranes.

True or False

If the statement is true, write "true." If it is false, change the underlined word or words to make the statement true.

1. Because they can find their way back to the beaches on which they hatched, sea turtles can be said to <u>migrate</u>.
2. The part of a reptile or bird egg that is the egg cell is the <u>egg white</u>.
3. Most <u>birds</u> have a double-loop circulatory system in which the loops are not completely separate.
4. Bird adaptations for flight include <u>hollow bones and egg-laying</u>.
5. <u>Alligators</u> have a narrow triangular snout and a toothy grin.
6. A(An) <u>bower</u> is an area in which an individual <u>animal</u> lives.
7. Snakes use their tongues to <u>sting</u>.
8. Songbirds are more correctly known as <u>birds of prey</u>.

Concept Mapping

Complete the following concept map for Section 4–1. Refer to pages C6–C7 to construct a concept map for the entire chapter.

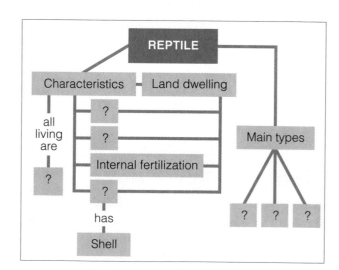

Concept Mastery

Discuss each of the following in a brief paragraph.

1. How are reptiles adapted to life on land?
2. Migration may be described as "animals traveling from where they breed to where they feed." How does this description relate to the behavior of sea turtles and many birds?
3. How is reproduction in birds adapted to the demands of flight?
4. What are the major structures of a typical reptile egg?
5. How do the respiratory and circulatory systems of a bird enable it to maintain a highly active lifestyle?
6. Racing pigeons are driven to a place many kilometers from their home and are then released. Even if they have never been at the starting point before, the birds head straight for home. How do the birds find their way back?
7. Parental care in animals ranges from virtually none to quite a lot. Using specific examples, explain how the behavior of reptiles and birds reflects this wide range of behaviors.
8. What is a territory? Why are territories important?

Critical Thinking and Problem Solving

Use the skills you have developed in this chapter to answer each of the following.

1. **Expressing an opinion** Because the skins of alligators, snakes, and some other reptiles make beautiful leather, many species have been hunted to the point of extinction. Do you think the hunting of reptiles should be allowed to continue? Should it be restricted? Should it be stopped altogether?
2. **Developing a hypothesis** Under what circumstances might a live-bearing bird evolve? Explain your reasoning.
3. **Relating concepts** The poisonous coral snake has alternating bands of black, bright red, and bright yellow. The harmless scarlet king snake has a very similar color pattern. Why is this distinctive pattern an advantage to the king snake?
4. **Evaluating theories** Some scientists say that fossil evidence strongly suggests that dinosaurs (long assumed to be coldblooded and an evolutionary dead end) were warmblooded and were the direct ancestors of birds. What sort of information would you need to better evaluate this two-part theory?

5. **Making inferences** In the spring and summer, male anoles (American chameleons) can be seen throwing their head back and thrusting out a flap of red skin from their throat. What do you think is the purpose of this behavior?
6. **Designing an experiment** A scientist wants to know whether turtles can detect sound. Design an experiment that she can use. Be sure to include a variable and a control in your experiment.
7. **Classifying animals** In the woods, you discover a small four-legged cold-blooded vertebrate. How can you tell whether it is an amphibian or a reptile?
8. **Using the writing process** Imagine that you are the reptile or bird of your choice. Write a short biography describing your life and times.

Mammals

A few hundred meters off the coast of California, a small group of animals swim playfully with one another. These whiskered animals are sea otters. A sea otter spends most of its life swimming in the cold waters of the North Pacific Ocean. While floating on its back, a sea otter often balances a rock on its chest. It is against this rock that the sea otter strikes a closed clam shell, cracking open the shell and eating the clam inside.

A sea otter appears to be an intelligent animal. To keep from being swept away by waves, a sea otter wraps itself in strands of giant seaweed growing offshore. It uses the seaweed as giant ropes are used to hold an ocean liner close to a pier.

Although sea otters spend a great deal of time in the water, they are neither fishes nor amphibians. Sea otters belong to the same group of warmblooded vertebrates that you do: the mammals. In addition to swimming in the sea, mammals can be found flying in the air and running along the ground. To learn more about these remarkable creatures, just turn the page.

Journal *Activity*

You and Your World If you have a pet mammal such as a dog, cat, hamster, rat, mouse, gerbil, horse, or guinea pig, observe it for a day. If you do not have a pet, observe one of your friend's pets. In your journal, record all the animal's activities and the time it spends doing each activity. Include a photograph of the animal in your journal.

◄ *A sea otter floating on strands of giant seaweed*

5–1 What Is a Mammal?

About 200 million years ago, the first mammals appeared on Earth. They evolved from a now-extinct group of reptiles. The first mammals were very small and looked something like the modern-day tree shrew shown in Figure 5–1.

Today there are about 4000 different kinds of mammals living on Earth. In addition to humans and sea otters, mammals include whales, bats, elephants, duckbill platypuses, lions, dogs, kangaroos, and monkeys. Because scientists group together animals with similar characteristics, you might wonder what such different-looking animals have in common.

Mammals have characteristics that set them apart from all other living things. **Mammals are warm-blooded vertebrates that have hair or fur and that feed their young with milk produced in mammary glands.** In fact, the word mammal comes from the term mammary gland. Another special characteristic of mammals is that they provide their young with more care and protection than do other animals.

At one time during their lives, all mammals possess fur or hair. If it is thick enough, the fur or hair acts as insulation and enables mammals such as musk oxen to survive in very cold parts of the world. Musk oxen are the furriest animals alive today. Indeed, the fur of an adult musk ox may be as deep as 15 centimeters! Mammals can also survive in harsh climates because they are warmblooded. Recall from Chapter 3 that warmblooded animals maintain their body temperatures internally as a result of the chemical reactions that occur within their cells. Thus mammals

Figure 5–1 *The first mammals to appear on Earth may have resembled the modern-day tree shrew (top). What characteristics common to all mammals are illustrated by the moose (bottom right) and the musk ox (bottom left)?*

maintain a constant body temperature despite the temperature of their surroundings. What other group of animals can do this?

All mammals, even those that live in the ocean, use their lungs to breathe. The lungs are powered by muscles—a group of muscles that are attached to the ribs and one large muscle that separates the abdomen from the chest.

The circulatory system of mammals consists of a four-chambered heart and an assortment of blood vessels. The heart pumps oxygen-poor blood to the lungs, where the blood exchanges its carbon dioxide for oxygen. After leaving the lungs, the oxygen-rich blood returns to the heart and is pumped to all parts of the body through blood vessels.

Mammals have the most highly developed excretory system of all the vertebrates. Paired kidneys filter nitrogen-containing wastes from the blood in the form of a substance called urea (yoo-REE-uh). Urea combines with water and other wastes to form urine. From the kidneys, urine travels to a urinary bladder, where it is stored until it passes out of the body.

The nervous system of mammals consists of a brain that is the most highly developed of all the animals. The brain makes thinking, learning, and understanding possible; coordinates movement; and regulates body functions. Mammals also have highly

ACTIVITY

DISCOVERING

Vertebrate Body Systems

Vertebrates have well-developed body systems that show considerable diversity from one group to another. Choose one of the systems listed below and illustrate how it changes from fishes to amphibians to reptiles to birds to mammals.

Systems: nervous system, digestive system, circulatory system, reproductive system, excretory system

■ Why do you think vertebrate systems become more complex?

Figure 5–2 *The large, flat, grinding teeth of a white-tailed deer indicate that this mammal eats plants. The sharp, pointed teeth of a gray wolf indicate that this mammal eats the flesh of its prey.*

Figure 5–3 *The brain of a mammal is large compared to that of other animals.*

developed senses that provide them with information about their environment. For example, humans, monkeys, gorillas, and chimpanzees are able to see objects in color. This characteristic is extremely useful because these mammals are most active during the day when their surroundings are bathed in light. Many mammals—cats, dogs, bats, and elephants, for example—are more sensitive to certain sounds than humans are.

Mammals also have more highly developed senses of taste and smell. For example, humans use both their sense of taste and their sense of smell to determine the flavor of food. Dogs and cats, as you might already know, recognize people by identifying specific body odors.

Like reptiles and birds, all mammals have internal fertilization, and males and females are separate individuals. However, the way in which mammals reproduce differs. The differences in reproduction

Figure 5–4 *The 4500 species of mammals can be divided into three main groups. What are the names of the three main groups?*

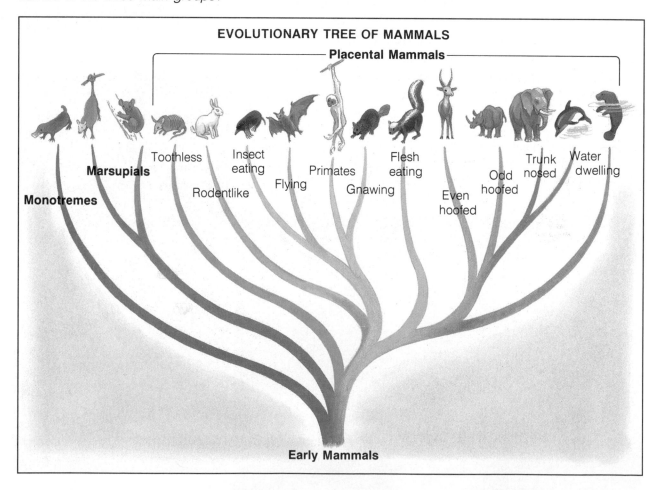

EVOLUTIONARY TREE OF MAMMALS

Placental Mammals

Monotremes
Marsupials
Toothless
Rodentlike
Insect eating
Flying
Primates
Gnawing
Flesh eating
Even hoofed
Odd hoofed
Trunk nosed
Water dwelling

Early Mammals

provide a means of classifying mammals into three main groups. These groups are **egg-laying mammals, pouched mammals,** and **placental** (pluh-SEHN-tuhl) **mammals.** Egg-laying mammals, as their name implies, lay eggs. Pouched mammals give birth to young that are not well developed. Thus the young must spend time in a pouchlike structure in their mother's body. In placental mammals, the young remain inside the mother until their body systems are able to maintain life on their own. At birth, these young are more developed than are those who spend time in their mother's pouch. You will learn more about each group of mammals in the remainder of this chapter.

5–1 Section Review

1. What are the main characteristics of mammals?
2. What is the function of mammary glands?
3. Classify the three groups of mammals.

Critical Thinking—*Relating Concepts*
4. Why does a mammal need more food during cold weather than during warmer weather?

5–2 Egg-Laying Mammals

One of the strangest looking mammals on the Earth today lives in rivers in isolated parts of Australia. It has fur as thick as a sea otter's, feet that are weblike and clawed, and a large flat ducklike beak! What is this strange creature?

If you look at Figure 5–5 on page 124, you will discover what this weird-looking animal is. It is a duckbill platypus. What makes the duckbill platypus stranger still is that although it is a mammal, it lays eggs! **Mammals that lay eggs are called egg-laying mammals, or monotremes** (MAHN-oh-treemz). Because of their ability to lay eggs, egg-laying mammals are sometimes referred to as reptilelike or primitive. The duckbill platypus and the spiny anteaters are the only known monotremes.

Guide for Reading

Focus on this question as you read.

▶ *What are egg-laying mammals?*

Figure 5–5 *The duckbill platypus (top) and the spiny anteater (bottom) are two of the six species of egg-laying mammals that exist today. Egg-laying mammals live in isolated parts of Australia and New Guinea. What is another name for egg-laying mammals?*

When a female duckbill platypus lays her soft marble-sized eggs, which usually number from one to three, she deposits them in a burrow she has dug in the side of a stream bank. The female will keep the eggs warm for the 10 days it takes them to hatch. Once hatched, the young platypuses are not left to find food for themselves (as are the young of reptiles). Instead, the young platypuses feed on milk produced by their mother's mammary glands, which are located on her abdomen. Milk production, as you may recall, is a characteristic of mammals.

Soon after a female spiny anteater lays her eggs, she places them into a pouch on her abdomen. The eggs hatch in 7 to 10 days. Like young platypuses, young spiny anteaters feed on milk produced by their mother's mammary glands.

The unusual body parts of a duckbill platypus help it to gather its food. For example, a duckbill platypus uses its claws to dig for insects, then uses its soft ducklike bill to scoop them up. The bill serves another important purpose: When under water, a platypus closes its eyes and ears. Unable to see as it swims above the riverbed, the platypus feels for snails, mussels, worms, and sometimes small fishes with its bill, which is very sensitive to touch.

Spiny anteaters also have special structures that help them to gather their food: ants and termites. A spiny anteater has a long, thin snout that it uses to probe for food, and it has a sticky, wormlike tongue that it flips out to catch insects. To protect itself, a spiny anteater uses its short powerful legs and curved claws to dig a hole in the ground and cover itself until only its spines are showing. These spines, which are 6 centimeters long, usually discourage almost any enemy.

5–2 Section Review

1. What is a characteristic of egg-laying mammals?
2. Name the two types of egg-laying mammals.

Critical Thinking—*Applying Concepts*
3. Why might egg-laying mammals be considered a link between reptiles and mammals?

5-3 Pouched Mammals

Unlike egg-laying mammals, pouched mammals do not lay eggs. Instead, they give birth to young that are not well developed. Thus the young must spend time in a pouchlike structure in their mother's body. Mammals that have pouches are called **marsupials** (mahr-soo-pee-uhlz).

When most people hear the word marsupial, they think of a kangaroo. Kangaroos, however, are not the only pouched mammals. Pouched mammals also include koalas, opossums, wombats, bandicoots, and gliders. Figure 5–6 shows some of these pouched mammals.

Perhaps the cuddliest and cutest pouched mammal is the koala. See Figure 5–7 on page 126. The koala's ears are big and round and covered with thick fur. Unlike many pouched mammals, a koala has a pouch whose opening faces its hind legs rather than its head. Koalas spend most of their time in trees, munching away on the only food they eat—the

Guide for Reading

Focus on these questions as you read.

▶ *What are pouched mammals?*

▶ *What are the similarities and differences between egg-laying mammals and pouched mammals?*

Figure 5–6 *The hairy-nosed wombat (bottom right), the eastern barred bandicoot (top left), and the sugar glider (bottom left) are examples of pouched mammals.*

leaves of eucalyptus trees. If you have ever smelled cough drops, you are probably familiar with the scent of eucalyptus leaves. The oils of the eucalyptus leaves are put into cough drops. So it is no wonder that koalas smell like cough drops! Because koalas eat only plant material, they, like most marsupials, are called herbivores (HER-buh-vorz).

Kangaroos

"At best it resembles a jumping mouse but it is much larger." These words were spoken in 1770 by the English explorer James Cook. He was describing an animal never before seen by Europeans. He later gave the name "kangaroo" to this strange animal.

Kangaroos live in the forests and grasslands of Australia. They have short front legs but long, muscular hind legs and tails. The tail helps the kangaroo to keep its balance and to push itself forward.

When a kangaroo is born, it is only 2 centimeters long and cannot hear or see. Although only partially developed at birth, it has front legs that enable it to crawl as many as 30 centimeters to its mother's pouch. To get a better idea of just what this feat involves, imagine the following: You are blindfolded, your ears are plugged, and you are placed in the center of a strange room about the size of half a football field. You are then told to find the exit on the first try! Obviously, this task is not easy. In fact, it is almost impossible. But the young kangaroo does it—and successfully, too. The young kangaroo, which is called a joey, stays in its mother's pouch for about 9 months, feeding on its mother's milk.

Figure 5–7 *Pouched mammals, such as the koala, the kangaroo, and the opossum, give birth to young that are not well developed. Thus the young must spend time in a pouchlike structure in their mother's body. Notice the baby kangaroo, called a joey, in its mother's pouch. What is another name for pouched mammals?*

Opossums

Have you ever heard the phrase "playing possum"? Do you know what it means? When in danger, opossums lie perfectly still, pretending to be dead. In some unknown way, this behavior helps to protect the opossum from its predators.

The opossum is the only pouched mammal found in North America. It lives in trees, often hanging onto branches with its long tail. Opossums eat fruits, insects, and other small animals.

Female opossums give birth to many opossums at one time. The females of one species of opossums, for example, give birth to as many as 56 offspring. Unfortunately, most of the newborn opossums do not survive the trip along their mother's abdomen to her pouch. Another species of female opossums produces newborns that are so tiny they have a mass of only 0.14 gram (about the mass of a small nail)!

Endangered Mammals

Endangered species are of concern to almost everyone. Using reference materials in the library, develop an ongoing list of endangered mammals. Be sure to include an illustration of each mammal on your list. Keep your list up to date.

What suggestions can you make to help prevent other mammals from becoming endangered species?

5–3 Section Review

1. What are pouched mammals? Give two examples of these mammals.
2. What is another name for a pouched mammal?
3. What is a herbivore?

Critical Thinking—*Applying Facts*
4. Explain why it is incorrect to refer to the koala as a koala bear.

5–4 Placental Mammals

Placental mammals give birth to young that remain inside the mother's body until their body systems are able to function independently. **Unlike the young of egg-laying and pouched mammals, the young of placental mammals develop more fully within the female.** The name for this group of mammals comes from a structure called a **placenta** (pluh-SEHN-tuh), which develops in females who are pregnant. Through the placenta, food, oxygen, and

Guide for Reading

Focus on these questions as you read.

▶ *What are placental mammals?*

▶ *What are ten major groups of placental mammals?*

Figure 5–8 *Placental mammals, such as the deer mouse, give birth to young that remain inside the mother's body until they can function on their own. What is the placenta?*

wastes are exchanged between the young and their mother. Thus the placenta allows the young to develop for a much longer time inside the mother.

The time the young spend inside the mother is called the **gestation** (jehs-TAY-shuhn) **period.** The gestation period in placental mammals ranges from a few weeks in mice to as long as 18 to 23 months in elephants. In humans, the gestation period is approximately 9 months. After female placental mammals give birth to their young, they supply the young with milk from their mammary glands. You should remember that this is a characteristic of all mammals.

There are many groups of placental mammals, organized here according to how they eat, how they move about, or where they live. Of these groups, 10 are discussed in the sections that follow.

Insect-Eating Mammals

What has a nose with 22 tentacles and spends half its time in water? The answer is a star-nosed mole. As you can see from Figure 5–9, a star-nosed mole gets its name from the ring of 22 tentacles on the end of its nose. No other mammal has this

Figure 5–9 *Insect-eating mammals include the star-nosed mole, the hedgehog, and the pygmy shrew. The star-nosed mole (top right) lives in moist or muddy soil in eastern parts of North America. The hedgehog (bottom right), which is covered by a thick coat of spines, curls into a ball when threatened. The pygmy shrew (bottom left) must eat twice its mass in insects every day to survive.*

structure. Each tentacle has very sensitive feelers, which enable a mole to find insects to eat and to feel its way around while burrowing under ground. Although star-nosed moles have eyes, the eyes are too tiny to see anything. They can only distinguish between light and darkness. A star-nosed mole spends one part of its day burrowing beneath the ground and the other part in the water.

In addition to moles, hedgehogs and shrews are also insect-eating mammals. Because it is covered with spines, a hedgehog looks like a walking cactus. When threatened by a predator, a hedgehog rolls up into a ball with only its spines showing. This action makes a hedgehog's enemy a little less enthusiastic about disturbing the tiny animal.

The pygmy shrew is the smallest mammal on Earth. As an adult, it has a mass of only 1.5 to 2 grams (about the mass of 10 small nails). Because shrews are so active, they must eat large amounts of food to maintain an adequate supply of energy. Shrews can eat twice their mass in insects every day!

Flying Mammals

Bats, which resemble mice, are the only flying mammals. In fact, the German word for bat is *Fledermaus,* which means flying mouse. Bats are able to fly because they have skin stretched over their arms and fingers, forming wings. Other mammals, such as flying squirrels, do not really fly. They simply glide to the ground after leaping from high places.

Although a bat's eyesight is poor, its hearing is excellent. While flying, a bat gives off high-pitched squeaks that people cannot hear. These squeaks bounce off nearby objects and return to the bat as echoes. By listening to these echoes, a bat knows just where objects are so that it can avoid them. Bats that hunt insects such as moths also use this method to locate their prey.

There are two main types of bats. Fruit-eating bats are found in tropical areas, such as Africa, Australia, India, and the Orient. Insect-eating bats live almost everywhere.

Figure 5–10 *Bats are the only flying mammals. A mouse-eared bat swoops down on its prey—a moth—while the long-tongued bat shows the feature for which it was named.*

The Fastest Runner

The cheetah, the fastest land animal, can run at speeds of up to 100 kilometers per hour. How far can it run in a second? In a minute?

Flesh-Eating Mammals

The frozen ice sheets and freezing waters of the Arctic are home to walruses. They are able to live in this harsh environment because they have a layer of fat, called blubber, under their skin. Blubber keeps body heat in. In addition to their large size, walruses have another noticeable feature: long tusks. These tusks are really special teeth called canines. Walrus canines can grow to 100 centimeters in length!

Walruses do not use their canines (tusks) for tearing and shredding food. Instead, they use their canines to open clams and to defend themselves from their predators: polar bears. Walruses also use their tusks as hooks to help them climb onto ice.

Figure 5–11 *Flesh-eating mammals such as the walrus, the tiger, the coyote, and the grizzly bear are placed in the same group. All these mammals have large pointed teeth that help them tear and shred flesh. What are some other examples of flesh-eating mammals?*

Like a walrus, you too have canines. However, your canines are not as large as a walrus's. You have a total of four canines: two in your upper set of teeth and two in your lower. To find your upper canines, look in a mirror and first locate your eight incisors, or front teeth—four on the bottom and four on top. Incisors are used to bite into food. On either side of your top and bottom incisors is a tooth that comes to a point. These teeth are your canines.

All flesh-eating mammals, including walruses, are known as carnivores (KAHR-nuh-vorz). Some carnivores live on land; others, such as walruses, live in the sea. Land carnivores such as cats, dogs, weasels, lions, wolves, and bears and their relatives have muscular legs that help them to chase other animals. These mammals also have sharp claws on their toes to help them hold their prey.

Like walruses, seals are flesh-eating mammals that live in the sea. The ancestors of these sea carnivores once lived on land but have since returned to the ocean, where they feed on fishes, mollusks (soft-bodied invertebrates that have inner or outer shells), and sea birds. The flipperlike arms and legs of seals, which are so useful in getting around in the water, make moving from place to place on land quite difficult. As a result, seals return to land only to breed and to give birth to their young.

Toothless Mammals

Although the name of this group indicates that its members do not have any teeth, there are some toothless mammals that actually do have small teeth. They include armadillos and sloths. The mammals in this group that actually have no teeth are the anteaters.

Unlike the spiny anteaters mentioned earlier in this chapter, the anteaters in this group do not lay eggs. As in all placental mammals, the young anteaters remain inside the female until they are more fully developed. However, both types of anteaters have something in common—a long sticky tongue that is used to catch insects. Look at Figures 5–5 and 5–12. Can you see any other similarities or differences between these two anteaters?

CAREERS
Veterinarian Assistant

Working on farms, in kennels, in hospitals, and in laboratories, **veterinarian assistants** are involved in health care for animals. They work under the supervision and instruction of a veterinarian. The duties of a veterinarian assistant include record keeping, specimen collection, laboratory work, and wound dressing. They also help with animals and equipment during surgery.

Patience, compassion, and a willingness to be involved with animal health care are important qualities for those interested in becoming a veterinarian assistant. To receive more information about this career, write to the American Veterinary Medical Association, 930 North Meacham Road, Schaumburg, IL 60196.

Figure 5–12 *Just as the name of their group implies, the true anteater (right) and the nine-banded armadillo (left) are toothless mammals.*

Armadillos, which live in parts of the southern United States and in Central and South America, eat plants, insects, and small animals. The most striking feature of an armadillo is its protective, armorlike coat. In fact, the word armadillo comes from a Spanish word that means armored. The nine-banded armadillo is the only toothless mammal found as far north as the United States.

Another type of toothless mammal is the sloth. There are two kinds of sloths: the two-toed sloth and the three-toed sloth. Sloths, which feed on leaves and fruits, are extremely slow-moving creatures. They spend most of their lives hanging upside down in trees. You may be amazed to learn that sloths can spend up to 19 hours a day resting in this position.

Trunk-Nosed Mammals

Figure 5–13 *The larger ears of the African elephant (bottom) distinguish it from the Indian elephant (top).*

As the elephant enters the river, it holds its trunk high in the air. Little by little, the water creeps up the elephant's body. Will it drown? The answer comes a few seconds later as the huge animal actually begins to swim!

To an observer on the shore, nothing can be seen of the elephant except its trunk, through which air enters on its way to the lungs. The trunk is the distinguishing feature of all elephants. Elephant trunks are powerful enough to tear large branches from trees. Yet they are agile enough to perform delicate movements, such as picking up a peanut thrown to them by a child at a zoo. These movements are made possible by the action of 40,000 muscles, which are controlled by a highly developed brain.

Elephants are the largest land animals. There are two kinds of elephants: African elephants and Asian elephants. As their names suggest, African elephants live in Africa and Asian elephants in Asia, especially in India and Southeast Asia. Although there are a number of differences between the two kinds of elephants, the most obvious one is ear size. The ears of African elephants are much larger than those of their Asian cousins.

Hoofed Mammals

What do pigs, camels, horses, and rhinoceroses have in common? Not much at first glance. In fact, they could not look more different. Yet if you were to take a closer look at their feet, you would see that they all have thick hoofs.

If you could take an even closer look at several hoofed mammals, you would discover that some have an even number of toes, whereas others have an odd number of toes. Pigs, camels, goats, cows, deer, and giraffes—the tallest of all mammals—have an even number of toes. Horses, rhinoceroses, zebras, hippopotamuses, and tapirs have an odd number of toes.

Hoofed mammals such as pigs, cows, deer, and horses are important to humans and have been so for thousands of years. These hoofed mammals provide humans with food and clothing, as well as with a means of transportation.

ACTIVITY

DISCOVERING

Migration of Mammals

Certain mammals migrate, or move, to places that offer better living conditions. Using posterboard and colored pencils, draw maps that trace the migration patterns of the following mammals: North American bat, African zebra, American elk, and gray whale. Display these maps on a bulletin board at school.

■ Why do you think each type of mammal migrates?

Figure 5–14 *A hippopotamus has an odd number of toes, whereas a giraffe has an even number of toes. Of what importance to people are hoofed mammals?*

Figure 5–15 *The most numerous mammals are the gnawing mammals. Two of the four special incisors that help gnawing mammals chew on hard objects such as wood and nuts can be seen in the photographs of the nutria (center) and the porcupine (bottom). Although the incisors of the chipmunk (top) are concealed by a mouthful of seeds, it too is a gnawing mammal.*

Gnawing Mammals

Hardly a day goes by that people in both the country and the city do not see a gnawing mammal. There are more gnawing mammals than there are any other type of mammal on the Earth. Gnawing mammals are more commonly known as rodents.

Among the rodents are such animals as squirrels, beavers, chipmunks, rats, mice, and porcupines. As you might expect, the characteristic that places these animals in the same group is the way they eat: They gnaw, or nibble. Gnawing mammals have four special incisors. These teeth are chisellike and continue to grow throughout the animal's lifetime. Because rodents gnaw on hard objects such as wood, nuts, and grain, their teeth get worn down as they grow. If this were not the case, a rodent's incisors would become so long that the animal would not be able to open its mouth wide enough to eat.

Some rodents, especially rats and mice, compete with humans for food. They eat the seeds of plants and many other foods used by people. Rodents are responsible for spreading more than 20 diseases, including bubonic plague—which is actually transmitted to people by the bite of a flea that lives on rats. Although it is no longer considered a serious disease, bubonic plague caused the deaths of 25 million people in Europe between the years 1300 and 1600.

Rodentlike Mammals

Rabbits, hares, and pikas (PIGH-kuhz) belong to the group known as rodentlike mammals. Like rodents, these mammals have gnawing teeth. Unlike rodents, however, they have a small pair of grinding teeth behind their gnawing teeth. Rodentlike mammals move their jaws from side to side as they chew their food, whereas rodents move their jaws from front to back.

Rabbits and hares have long hind legs that are used for quick movement and flight from danger. Some larger hares can reach speeds of up to 80 kilometers per hour! In addition, rabbits and hares have large eyes that enable them to remain active during the night.

How are hares and rabbits different? In terms of appearance, hares tend to have longer legs and longer ears than rabbits do. Hares also live on their own on the surface of the ground. Rabbits are born in burrows and are helpless for the first few weeks of their lives.

Pikas, which have large rounded ears and short legs, are not well known because they live high up in the mountains or below ground in burrows. If you are interested in seeing a pika, look at Figure 5–16.

Water-Dwelling Mammals

"Thar she blows!" is the traditional cry of a sailor who spots the fountain of water that a whale sends skyward just before it dives. Although sailors of the past recognized this sign of a whale, they had no idea that this sea animal was a mammal, not a fish.

Whales, porpoises, dolphins, dugongs, and manatees are water-dwelling mammals. Although they live in water most or all of the time, they have lungs and breathe air. They feed their young with milk and have hair at some time in their life.

Whales, dolphins, and porpoises spend their entire lives in the ocean and cannot survive on land. Dugongs and manatees live in shallower water, often in rivers and canals. Because of their large size, it is difficult for dugongs and manatees to move around on land. However, they do so for short periods of time when they become stranded.

Figure 5–16 *The pika (top) and the rabbit (bottom) belong to the group known as the rodentlike mammals.*

Figure 5–17 *Two examples of mammals that live in water are the manatee (left) and the humpback whale (right). What are some other examples of water-dwelling mammals?*

Figure 5–18 *Of all the animals, primates, such as the gibbon (top), the chimpanzee (center), and the orangutan (bottom), have the most highly developed brain and the most complicated behaviors. What are some other characteristics of primates?*

Primates

On a visit to your local zoo, you come upon a crowd of people gathered in front of one of the cages. Hurrying over to see what the excitement is about, you hear strange noises. Carefully you make your way to the front of the crowd, where you see what is causing all the commotion. A family of chimpanzees is entertaining the crowd by running and tumbling about in their cage. The baby chimpanzee comes to the front of the cage and extends its hand to you. You are amazed to see how much like your hand the chimpanzee's hand looks. But it is really no wonder they are similar. After all, the chimpanzee—along with the gibbon (GIHB-uhn), orangutan (oh-RANG-oo-tan), and gorilla—is the closest mammal in structure to humans.

These mammals, along with baboons, monkeys, and humans, belong to the same group—the primates. All primates have eyes that face forward, enabling the animals to see depth. Primates also have five fingers on each hand and five toes on each foot. The fingers are capable of very complicated movements, such as the ability to grasp objects.

Primates also have large brains and are considered the most intelligent mammals. Chimpanzees can be taught to communicate with people by using sign language. Some scientists have reported that chimpanzees can use tools, such as when they use twigs to remove insects from a log. Humans, on the other hand, are the only primates that can make their own tools.

5–4 Section Review

1. What are placental mammals? What is the function of a placenta?
2. What is a gestation period?
3. How do a carnivore and a herbivore differ?
4. List ten groups of placental mammals and give an example of each group.

Connection—*Ecology*

5. Elephants often use their tusks to strip the bark from trees. How might this action harm the environment?

CONNECTIONS

Do You Hear What I Hear?

The question posed in the title is really not so easily answered. If you were a cat, dog, porpoise, or bat—and you could speak—you would have four different answers to this question. Why? Each one of these mammals is capable of hearing sounds other animals cannot!

Sound is a form of energy that is produced when particles vibrate. The number of particle vibrations per second, or the frequency, is an important characteristic of sound. The ear can respond only to certain frequencies. For example, the normal human ear is capable of detecting sounds that have between 20 and 20,000 vibrations per second. Sounds with frequencies higher than 20,000 vibrations per second are called *ultrasonic sounds* (the prefix *ultra-* means beyond). Ultrasonic sounds cannot be heard by the human ear.

Some animals can hear ultrasonic sounds, however. If you have ever used a dog whistle, you know that when you blow on it, your dog comes running even though you cannot hear any sound. Dogs can hear sounds that have frequencies up to 25,000 vibrations per second. Cats can hear sounds with frequencies up to 65,000 vibrations per second. The frequency limit for porpoises is 150,000 vibrations per second. And bats can hear ultrasonic sounds with frequencies up to 200,000 vibrations per second. Bats not only hear ultrasonic sounds, they also produce ultrasonic sounds. They use the echoes to avoid bumping into things and to locate prey such as moths. This process of navigation is called *echolocation.* The echolocation of many bats is so efficient that they can make last-minute swerves in order to intercept a moth that has changed its course!

Laboratory Investigation

Examining Hair

Problem

What are the characteristics of hair?

Materials *(per student)*

medicine dropper	coverslip
methylene blue	microscope
glass slide	electric light
comb or brush	hand lens
scissors	

Procedure 🔺 ▧ ⊫ ☒

1. Using the medicine dropper, put 2 drops of methylene blue in the center of a clean glass slide. **CAUTION:** *Be careful when using methylene blue because it may stain your skin and clothing.*

2. Comb or brush your hair vigorously to remove a few loose hairs.

3. From your comb or brush, select two hairs that each have a root attached. The root is the small bulb-shaped swelling at one end of the hair.

4. Using the scissors, trim the other end of each hair so it will be short enough to fit on the glass slide. Place the trimmed hairs in the drops of methylene blue on the slide. Cover the slide.

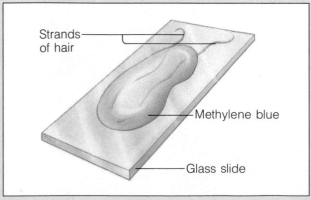

Strands of hair

Methylene blue

Glass slide

5. Use the low-power objective of the microscope to locate the hairs. Then switch to the high-power objective and focus with the fine adjustment. Make a sketch of the hair strand.

6. Turn the fine adjustment toward you (counterclockwise) to focus on the upper surface of the hair. At one point in your focusing, the hair will appear to be covered by overlapping structures that look like shingles. Draw these structures, which are actually cells.

7. Under bright light, use the hand lens to examine a portion of your skin that does not seem to be covered with hair. (Do not examine the palms of your hands or the soles of your feet.)

Observations

1. Describe the appearance of a strand of hair under the microscope.

2. Describe the appearance of cells covering the strand of hair.

3. What did you observe when you examined the surface of your skin under bright light?

Analysis and Conclusions

1. Based on your observations, what is hair?

2. **On Your Own** Obtain hair from several of the pets mentioned in the Journal Activity at the beginning of the chapter. Prepare these hair samples as you did your hair sample. Compare the various hair samples. Are they about the same thickness as your hair when observed with the unaided eye? When observed with the microscope? What other similarities or differences do you observe?

Summarizing Key Concepts

5–1 What Is a Mammal?

▲ Mammals are warmblooded vertebrates that have hair or fur and that feed their young with milk produced in mammary glands.

▲ Mammals use their lungs to breathe. Their circulatory system consists of a four-chambered heart and blood vessels. Paired kidneys filter nitrogen-containing wastes from the blood in the form of urea. Urea, water, and other wastes form urine, which is stored in the urinary bladder.

▲ Mammals have well-developed brains and senses, and they have internal fertilization.

▲ Mammals can be placed into three basic groups depending on the way in which they reproduce. These groups are the egg-laying mammals, the pouched mammals, and the placental mammals.

5–2 Egg-Laying Mammals

▲ Mammals that lay eggs are called egg-laying mammals, or monotremes.

▲ The duckbill platypus and the spiny anteater are examples of egg-laying mammals.

5–3 Pouched Mammals

▲ Unlike monotremes, pouched mammals do not lay eggs. Instead, they give birth to young that are not well developed. Thus the young must spend time in a pouchlike structure in their mother's body. Mammals that have pouches are called marsupials.

5–4 Placental Mammals

▲ Placental mammals give birth to young that remain inside the mother's body until their body systems are able to function independently. The placenta is a structure through which food, oxygen, and wastes are exchanged between the young and their mother.

▲ Insect-eating mammals include moles, hedgehogs, and shrews.

▲ Bats are the only flying mammals.

▲ Flesh-eating mammals, or carnivores, include sea-living animals such as walruses and seals. Land-living carnivores include any members of the dog, cat, and bear families.

▲ Toothless mammals include those animals that lack teeth or have small teeth.

▲ The only members of the trunk-nosed mammal group are the elephants.

▲ Hoofed mammals are divided into the group that has an even number of toes on each hoof and the group that has an odd number of toes.

▲ Gnawing mammals, such as beavers, chipmunks, rats, mice, and porcupines, have chisellike incisors for chewing.

▲ Rabbits, hares, and pikas are examples of rodentlike mammals.

▲ Mammals such as whales, dolphins, porpoises, dugongs, and manatees are water-dwelling mammals.

▲ Humans, monkeys, and apes are primates.

Reviewing Key Concepts

Define each term in a complete sentence.

5–1 What Is a Mammal?
egg-laying mammal
pouched mammal
placental mammal

5–4 Placental Mammals
placenta
gestation period

Chapter Review

Content Review

Multiple Choice

Choose the letter of the answer that best completes each statement.

1. All mammals have
   a. pouches.
   b. hair.
   c. feathers.
   d. fins.
2. The kangaroo is a(n)
   a. pouched mammal.
   b. egg-laying mammal.
   c. placental mammal.
   d. gnawing mammal.
3. The only North American marsupial is the
   a. kangaroo.
   b. koala.
   c. platypus.
   d. opossum.
4. Young mammals that develop totally within the female belong to the group called
   a. egg-laying mammals.
   b. pouched mammals.
   c. placental mammals.
   d. marsupial mammals.
5. Which is an insect-eating mammal?
   a. whale
   b. elephant
   c. bear
   d. mole

6. Which teeth are used to tear and shred food?
   a. carnivores
   b. canines
   c. incisors
   d. herbivores
7. Which is an example of a toothless mammal?
   a. skunk
   b. mole
   c. armadillo
   d. camel
8. The largest land animal is the
   a. blue whale.
   b. rhinoceros.
   c. elephant.
   d. giraffe.
9. An example of a water-dwelling mammal is the
   a. spiny anteater.
   b. dolphin.
   c. shrew.
   d. elephant.
10. To which group of mammals do humans belong?
    a. insect-eating mammals
    b. rodents
    c. primates
    d. carnivores

True or False

If the statement is true, write "true." If it is false, change the underlined word or words to make the statement true.

1. Mammals are <u>invertebrates</u>.
2. Mammals are <u>warmblooded</u> animals.
3. The duckbill platypus is an example of a <u>marsupial</u>.
4. Animals that eat only plants are called <u>herbivores</u>.
5. The <u>gestation period</u> is the time the young of placental mammals spend inside their mother.
6. Rabbits are <u>gnawing</u> mammals.
7. Carnivore means <u>flesh eater</u>.
8. Humans are <u>primates</u>.

Concept Mapping

Complete the following concept map for Section 5–1. Refer to pages C6–C7 to construct a concept map for the entire chapter.

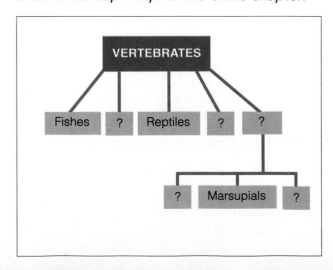

Concept Mastery

Discuss each of the following in a brief paragraph.

1. What are the characteristics of mammals? What are the three groups of mammals? How do they differ from one another?
2. What is the difference between an anteater and a spiny anteater?
3. Name two pouched mammals. Explain how their young develop.
4. What are mammary glands?
5. List ten groups of placental mammals and give an example of each.
6. Why are whales considered mammals and not fishes?
7. What features make carnivores good predators?
8. Why are primates considered the most intelligent mammals?

Critical Thinking and Problem Solving

Use the skills you have developed in the chapter to answer each of the following.

1. **Relating facts** Which group of mammals is most similar to birds? Explain your answer.
2. **Making charts** Prepare a chart with three columns. In the first column, list the ten groups of mammals that you learned about in this chapter. In the second column, list the characteristics of each group. And in the third column, list at least two examples of each group.
3. **Applying concepts** Why do whales usually come to the surface of the ocean several times an hour?
4. **Making inferences** Many species of hoofed mammals feed in large groups, or herds. What advantage could this behavior have for the survival of these mammals?
5. **Making generalizations** What is the relationship between how complex an animal is and the amount of care the animal gives to its young? Provide an example to support your answer.
6. **Designing an experiment** Design an experiment that will test the following hypothesis: Chimpanzees are able to understand the meaning of the spoken words for the numbers 1 through 10.
7. **Using the writing process** Imagine that you are a writer for a wildlife magazine. Your boss tells you that she has decided not to include mammals in the magazine because she finds them dull. Write a memo to change her mind. Include the characteristics that separate mammals from other animals.

GAZETTE

MICHAEL WERIKHE

Saving the Rhino—One Step at a Time

There are few animals as impressive as a rhinoceros. Roughly 4 meters long from head to tail and about 2300 kilograms in mass, a large rhino is approximately the size of a small car. A rhino's enormous size, beady eyes, armored skin, curving horn (or horns), and stocky legs remind some people of the dinosaurs that roamed the Earth long ago.

Recently, it became apparent that rhinos were in great danger of sharing yet another characteristic with dinosaurs: being extinct. (The word extinct is used to describe a type of living thing that has died out completely and vanished forever.) Why? Because in the past 20 years, more than 90 percent of the world's rhinos have been killed for their horns.

African rhinos have two horns: a long one on the tip of their snout and a smaller one behind it. Asian rhinos have only one horn. In both types of rhinos, the horns are nothing more than large curved cones made of the same substance as your fingernails. But in some parts of the world, people believe that rhino horns have magical properties. In Yemen, for example, rhino horns are used to make the handles of special daggers. And in China, ground-up rhino horns are used in "medicines" for fevers and other ailments.

What can be done to stop the slaughter of the rhinos before it's too late? Groups of nations have agreed to prohibit trade in rhino horns. Individual countries have made rhino hunting illegal, set up protected wildlife parks, and supplied park rangers with better equipment for stopping illegal hunters. Zoos have developed ways of raising and breeding rhinos in captivity. And Michael Werikhe (WAIR-ree-kee), a young man from Kenya, has walked more than 7800 kilometers to make people aware of the threat to rhinos and to raise money for rhino conservation programs.

Michael Werikhe is not a politician, scientist, or professional fundraiser. He is a

security officer at an auto factory, and he doesn't particularly like to walk. But he is determined to do all he can to save rhinos from extinction.

As a boy, Werikhe played in the mangrove forests and explored the seashore near his home city of Mombasa. These childhood activities filled him with a deep appreciation for the living world. After high school, he took a government job that he thought might be related to his interest in wildlife. But it was not quite what he expected. He worked in a government warehouse that stored elephant tusks and rhinoceros horns confiscated from illegal hunters or collected from animals that had to be killed by game wardens. Werikhe's job was to sort these grisly trophies so that the government could sell them at auctions. Although Werikhe soon quit, the memory of the tusks, horns, and wasted wildlife they represented remained with him.

When Werikhe quit his job at the government warehouse, there were about 20,000 black rhinos in Kenya. Ten years later, there were about 500. To Werikhe, the rhinos became a symbol of all the threatened wildlife he loved. He had to do something. So he walked from Mombasa to Nairobi, a journey of about 480 kilometers. On his way, he stopped at many small villages and talked to people about the dangers rhinos faced.

"Too often, wildlife professionals assume that the average African cares little about preserving his natural heritage," Werikhe notes. "In my walks I've found that people *do* care, but feel left out."

In 1985, with the support of his employer and his fellow workers, Werikhe left his job and set off on a nearly 2100-kilometer trek across Africa. Three years later, he was off on another transcontinental hike. This time the continent was Europe. The walk raised $1 million for rhino conservation.

From April through September 1991, Werikhe, then 34 years old, undertook his third marathon walk. This walk took him to Washington, DC, Dallas, Toronto, San Diego, and many other major cities in North America. Three fourths of the approximately $2 million that he raised was for rhino programs in Africa; the rest was for rhino programs in North American zoos.

Werikhe has been honored for his work with a number of prestigious environmental

▲▼ In some parts of the world, people believe that rhino horns possess magical properties. As a result, African rhinos (top) and Indian rhinos (bottom) are in danger of becoming extinct.

awards, including the United Nations Environment Program's Global 500 Award. He has shown the world that the efforts of one ordinary person (with extraordinary determination) can go a long way toward solving global problems. But the accomplishment that might mean the most to Michael Werikhe is this: Thanks in large part to his efforts, the African rhino population seems to be back on the road to recovery.

TUNA NET FISHING:

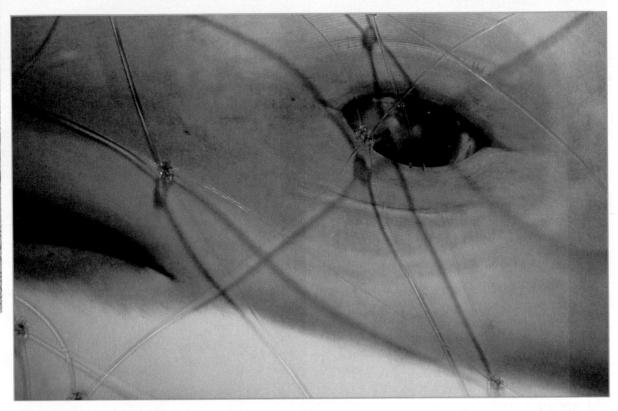

DOLPHINS IN DANGER!

Sorry, Charlie! Although tuna fish, whether in a sandwich, in a salad, or on a plate, remains a popular meal, some tuna-fishing methods are now considered unacceptable. Why is this so? Environmentalists have shown that purse seines, the very large rectangular fishing nets used to catch most tuna, have also caught and destroyed as many as 80,000 to 100,000 dolphins a year for the past several years. Fishing regulations permit a certain number of dolphins to be killed as a result of commercial fish-

ing. However, the actual number of dolphin deaths is four to five times greater than that allowed by law.

Most tuna fishing takes place in the Pacific Ocean, where fishing boats from the United States as well as from the Republic of Korea, Taiwan, and Japan enjoy access to the fish-rich waters. There, fishers often find schools of yellow-fin tuna swimming with dolphins. In fact, fishers rely on the dolphins to help them locate large quantities of tuna. But the fishers' nets cannot tell the difference between fishes and mammals. The

◄▲ **When dolphins are caught in nets (right), they cannot surface for air and they drown. Fortunately, this dolphin (left) was freed by a diver swimming nearby.**

purse seines trap both tunas and dolphins under water. Unable to surface for their much-needed air, the dolphins drown.

Purse seines are not the only fishing equipment responsible for the deaths of vast numbers of marine life. Drift nets, which are huge fishing nets that placed together can stretch more than 4 kilometers across, have also produced criticism from scientists. Drift nets have been used to catch a wide variety of commercial species—including cod, tuna, and squid—since the late 1970s. But because of their size, drift nets ensnare and kill a tremendous number of other species of marine life, such as sharks, dolphins, sea turtles, and sea birds. In the last half of 1989, an estimated 1.5 million blue sharks, 23,000 dolphins, and 230,000 sea birds were killed in drift nets. The nets may also be responsible for reducing some of the commercial fish supply beyond a healthy number, thus interfering with the development of young fishes. So although scientists still do not have all the data they need to completely assess the situation, they are expressing alarm at the threat the drift nets may pose to marine ecosystems.

Scientists are not the only people concerned with purse seines and drift nets. The general public as well as national and international governing bodies have been part of a global effort to protect dolphins—as well as other types of marine life—from the nets. For instance, various concerned people—including schoolchildren—used boycotts and crusades to convince three major American tuna marketers to stop buying tuna from fishing companies that used purse seines. Tuna marketers now put special labels on their cans to show that the tuna inside was caught by relatively "dolphin-safe" methods.

In 1990, the United Nations passed a resolution that would prohibit drift-net fishing in the South Pacific by 1991 and worldwide by 1992. The resolution, however, leaves room for drift-netters: They will be allowed to use their nets if they take "effective conservation and management measures." These measures include releasing the marine life that accidentally gets trapped in the nets.

△ **Leaping dolphins have captivated people's imagination for centuries.**

Ocean is harvested in ways that provide a minimal threat to dolphins.

Officials from various countries also fear for the economic safety of their businesses and workers. Safer nets will not only cost more money, they will also increase competition by limiting the availability of fishing sites. And in the end, it will be the consumers who will feel these effects by having to pay a higher price for the tuna.

Fishing practices and the responsibilities of people to protect water wildlife have sparked debate in homes, classrooms, and national and international congresses. What do you think?

But some environmental groups are still worried. They fear that because the nets catch such a wide variety of marine species, it may be impossible to take the effective measures necessary to protect all the species.

Meanwhile, other groups are responding to the fishing restrictions in other ways. Members of the tuna-fishing industry argue that companies refusing to do business with fishers who use purse seines may actually end up doing more harm than good. They explain that fishers will be forced to catch mostly the young tuna that do not swim with dolphins. This action would ultimately reduce the supply of tuna. And they add that the cruelty of their industry is highly exaggerated. In fact, they claim that 90 percent of the tuna caught in the Pacific

▽ **The label "dolphin safe" indicates that the tuna inside this can was not caught in nets that also kill dolphins.**

The *HIT* of the Class of 2025

Hidden in the blood of hibernating animals is a newly discovered chemical. It could slow the aging process of humans and make years-long journeys into space possible.

The wallscreen glowed faintly as George sat quietly at his television console. His heart pounded faster and faster as he heard the announcer's voice. "T minus five minutes and counting."

The picture on the screen showed the largest spaceship ever built on Earth. Inside, a team of astronauts was prepared for

▲ Ground squirrels enter a state of hibernation during the cold winter months.

the longest space journey ever attempted by humans—a five-year trip to the outer planets and their moons. The astronauts planned to "sleep" through most of the trip as automatic devices guided the spaceship to its destination. But how could humans sleep for days, weeks, even months without eating or drinking?

The answer, which George knew, was simple. The astronauts would hibernate! During hibernation, their body temperatures would be lowered. All their bodily activities would slow down considerably, which is exactly what happens to the bodies of hibernating animals such as squirrels and dormice.

But, you might think, people do not hibernate. Well, not now, but by the year 2025 . . .

GETTING HIT MAKES SENSE

"As you know," the announcer said, "the astronauts will soon inject themselves with a substance called hibernation-induction trigger, or HIT for short. This substance was discovered in the blood of hibernating animals back in the 1970s. Perhaps more startling, when HIT first was injected into nonhibernating animals, the animals promptly went to sleep. Now that HIT has been developed for use in humans, astronauts can be sent on spaceflights that take months or years. They'll just sleep through the flights. They won't get bored or need food."

George thought about other ways in which HIT could be used. For example, scientists had discovered about 40 years earlier that cancer does not spread in hibernating animals. This means that cancer patients could be put into a state of hibernation while receiving special treatments. Also, a hibernating body can take much more stress than an active body can. So patients could be placed in hibernation during surgery. This would eliminate the risks involved in using drugs to put patients to sleep. In addition, because bodies age very little while hibernating, people's lives could be extended considerably if they hibernated from time to time.

This last thought threw George a bit. "I don't know if I'd want to live longer if I had to sleep away every winter like a squirrel," he thought to himself. "I'd miss skiing and ice skating and . . . " George's thoughts were interrupted by his older sister's voice.

"It's two o'clock, George. Aren't you going to the senior barbecue?"

"I almost forgot!" George exclaimed as he leaped out of his chair and headed for the door.

"How could you forget the farewell party for the Class of 2025?" his sister teased as George dashed out of the house.

Behind George, the wallscreen still glowed. Suddenly, a huge flaming cloud of gas burst from the bottom of the rocket shown on the screen. Gaining speed with each passing second, the rocket rose faster and faster, launching its crew on the first leg of its five-year mission. The astronauts would return feeling and looking only about one year older! HIT would help keep them young.

STAYING YOUNGER

As George arrived at the barbecue, his mind wandered back to the scene on the wallscreen and the announcer's description of HIT. Again his thoughts were interrupted by a voice.

"Here's to the reunion of 2050," called one of George's friends.

"And to the one in 2075," cried another friend. The class had decided that no matter how far its members would wander, they would all get together every 25 years.

"Ugh," groaned still another friend, "we'll all be old, wrinkled, and gray by then."

"Maybe not," George said with a smile.

"What are you talking about?" asked a number of friends at the same time.

George paused for a moment in order to build up the suspense.

"What if we were able to hibernate for eight hours a day instead of sleeping for the same amount of time?"

"We'd turn into squir-rels," joked someone, causing everyone to laugh.

"Not quite," said George. "We just might not turn into old people as fast as we would normally."

"I don't get it," stated a classmate.

"Simple," said George. "Eight hours is a third of a day. If we didn't age—or, at least didn't age much—for a third of the time, we'd only age about 18 years out of every 25."

"You mean in 2050 I'd look like 36 instead of 43?" came a question from the crowd.

"Maybe. And in 2075 you'd look like you were in your early fifties instead of your late sixties."

"Is it really possible?" someone asked.

A blur of gray fur caught George's eye as he was about to answer. The blur raced up the side of a nearby tree. George stared at the little animal with the bushy tail.

"You might ask the squirrel," suggested George. "He knows the secret."

▼ **These people—all of whom are at least 100 years old—live in certain areas in Russia. Scientists wonder why.**

For Further Reading

If you have been intrigued by the concepts examined in this textbook, you may also be interested in the ways fellow thinkers—novelists, poets, essayists, as well as scientists—have imaginatively explored the same ideas.

Chapter 1: Sponges, Cnidarians, Worms, and Mollusks

Headstrom, Richard. *Suburban Wildlife*. Englewood Cliffs, NJ: Prentice Hall.

Henry, O. "The Octopus Marooned." In *The Complete Works of O. Henry*. New York: Doubleday.

Rockwell, Thomas. *How to Eat Fried Worms*. New York: Franklin Watts.

Sroda, George. *Life Story of TV Star and Celebrity Herman the Worm*. Amherst Junction, WI: G. Sroda.

Terris, Susan. *Octopus Pie*. New York: Farrar, Straus & Giroux.

Chapter 2: Arthropods and Echinoderms

Fleischman, Paul. *Joyful Noise: Poems for Two Voices*. New York: Harper & Row.

Goor, Ron, and Nancy Goor. *Insect Metamorphosis: From Egg to Adult*. New York: Atheneum.

Herberman, Ethan. *The Great Butterfly Hunt: The Mystery of the Migrating Monarchs*. New York: Simon & Schuster.

Kingsley, Charles. *The Water-babies*. New York: Dodd, Mead.

Kipling, Rudyard. *Just So Stories*. New York: Harper & Row.

Webster, Jean. *Daddy Long-Legs*. New York: Scholastic.

White, E. B. *Charlotte's Web*. New York: Harper & Row Junior Books.

Chapter 3: Fishes and Amphibians

Cole, Harold. *A Few Thoughts on Trout*. New York: Messner.

Dobrin, Arnold. *Going to Moscow and Other Stories*. New York: Four Winds.

East, Ben. *Trapped in Devil's Hole*. Riverside, NY: Crestwood.

George, Jean Craighead. *Shark Beneath the Reef*. New York: Harper & Row.

Kipling, Rudyard. *Captains Courageous*. New York: Airmont.

Chapter 4: Reptiles and Birds

Aesop. *Aesop's Fables*. New York: Avenel Books.

Blotnick, Elihu. *Blue Turtle Moon Queen*. Canyon, CA: California Street Press.

Edler, Timothy J. *Maurice the Snake and Gaston the Nearsighted Turtle*. Loreauville, LA: Little Cajun Books.

Fleischman, Paul. *I Am Phoenix: Poems for Two Voices*. New York: Harper & Row.

Henry, O. "A Bird of Baghdad." In *The Complete Works of O. Henry*. New York: Doubleday.

Lavies, Bianca. *The Secretive Timber Rattlesnake*. New York: Dutton.

Yolen, Jane. *Bird Watch: A Book of Poetry*. New York: Philomel.

Chapter 5: Mammals

Bowman, James Cloyd, and Margery Bianco. *Tales from a Finnish Tupa*. Chicago, IL: Albert Whitman.

Burnford, Sheila. *The Incredible Journey*. Boston, MA: Little, Brown.

George, Jean Craighead. *Julie of the Wolves*. New York: Harper & Row.

Kipling, Rudyard. *The Jungle Book*. New York: New American Library.

Nash, Ogden. *The Animal Garden*. New York: M. Evans.

Patent, Dorothy Hinshaw. *Seals, Sea Lions, and Walruses*. New York: Holiday House.

Rawlings, Marjorie Kinnan. *The Yearling*. New York: Macmillan.

ctivity Bank

Welcome to the Activity Bank! This is an exciting and enjoyable part of your science textbook. By using the Activity Bank you will have the chance to make a variety of interesting and different observations about science. The best thing about the Activity Bank is that you and your classmates will become the detectives, and as with any investigation you will have to sort through information to find the truth. There will be many twists and turns along the way, some surprises and disappointments too. So always remember to keep an open mind, ask lots of questions, and have fun learning about science.

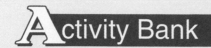
TO CLASSIFY OR NOT TO CLASSIFY?

Have you ever tried to organize the clothes in your room? If so, perhaps you put all your sweaters into one group, your socks into another group, and your jeans into still another group. In other words, you classified your clothes into specific groups based on their common characteristics. Why is it useful to classify objects? Try this activity and find out.

Part A. You will need 26 index cards and a pencil for this activity.

What Do You Need to Do?

1. Write each letter of the alphabet on an index card. Use only capital letters.
2. Choose any trait that will enable you to classify the letters. Arrange the letters in their appropriate groups.
3. After you have classified the letters according to one trait, choose another trait and again classify the letters into groups.

Index cards

What Did You Find Out?

1. What traits did you use to classify the letters of the alphabet?
2. How were the letters arranged in each group?

Part B. Now try your hand at classifying living things. You will need 20 photographs of plants for this activity.

What Do You Need to Do?

1. Collect 20 photographs of plants.
2. Classify the plants according to color.
3. Then classify the plants according to whether they live in water or on land.
4. Examine the photographs of the plants again. Determine whether another trait will help you classify the plants. Arrange the plants in their appropriate groups.
5. After you have classified the plants into their specific groups, name each group based on the trait that best describes it.
6. Give your photographs of the plants to a classmate and tell your classmate the names you have given each group. Have your classmate use your group names to classify the photographs. Then switch roles and try to do the same with your classmate's group names.

What Did You Find Out?

1. Is color a good way to classify plants? Explain your answer.
2. Is where a plant lives a good trait to use in classifying plants?
3. Did you and your classmate match each other's photographs with the appropriate group names?
4. Did either of you have any difficulty in doing so? If either of you did, what changes could be made in order to match the group name with the appropriate photograph?
5. Can you think of other traits that may be better for classifying plants?
6. Why do you think it is helpful to classify objects?

FRIENDS OR FOES?

Do animals and plants need each other? Can they survive without one another? Try this activity to find out the answers to these questions.

What Will You Need?

small plastic bag with a twist tie
distilled water
medicine dropper
bromthymol blue solution
pond snail
Elodea sprig

What Will You Do?

1. Fill a plastic bag two-thirds full with distilled water.

2. Put a few drops of bromthymol blue solution into the plastic bag to make the water blue.

3. Put a pond snail into the plastic bag. Seal the bag with a twist tie and put it in a place where it will remain undisturbed for 20 minutes.

4. After 20 minutes, observe the color of the water. Bromthymol blue solution will turn yellow in the presence of carbon dioxide.

5. Unseal the plastic bag and add an *Elodea* sprig. Reseal the plastic bag and place it in an area that receives light (not direct sunlight) for 20 minutes.

6. After 20 minutes, observe any changes in the color of the water.

What Did You See?

1. What was the color of the water containing the pond snail after 20 minutes?

2. What was the color of the water containing the pond snail and *Elodea* sprig after 20 minutes?

What Did You Discover?

1. What happened to the carbon dioxide gas that was produced by the snail?

2. Do animals and plants need each other? Explain.

3. Many trees in the Amazon rain forest are being destroyed to clear the land for farming and ranching. Explain how the disappearance of the rain forest would affect the gases in the environment.

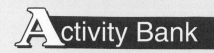
MOVING AT A SNAIL'S PACE

After insects, mollusks are the most varied group of animals on the Earth. Most mollusks have bodies that are covered by a shell. This activity will help you become more familiar with one small member of this group—a pond snail.

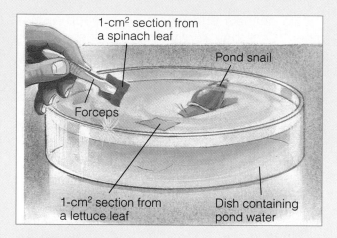

1-cm^2 section from a spinach leaf

Pond snail

Forceps

1-cm^2 section from a lettuce leaf

Dish containing pond water

Materials

large dish	forceps
pond water	paper towel
pond snail	microscope slide
scissors	clock with second
metric ruler	indicator
lettuce and	2 cm x 6 cm piece
spinach leaves	of sandpaper

Procedure

1. Half fill the large dish with pond water and place the pond snail in the dish.

2. With the scissors, cut a 1-cm^2 section from the lettuce leaf and from the spinach leaf. Put the leaf squares in the dish with the pond snail.

3. Place the dish containing the pond snail and leaf squares in a place where they will remain undisturbed for 24 hours.

4. After 24 hours, remove the leaf squares from the dish and place them on the paper towel to remove excess water. Note how much of each square has been eaten.

5. Arrange the microscope slide in the dish so that the slide leans at a 45° angle against the side of the dish.

6. Place the snail at the top of the slide.

7. Measure the time it takes the snail to travel down and then up the microscope slide. Record the time for each.

8. Cover the microscope slide with the piece of sandpaper and repeat steps 5 through 7.

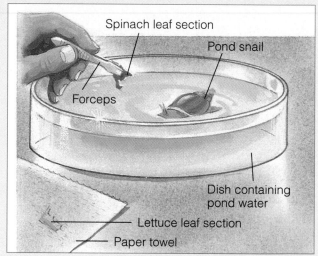

Spinach leaf section

Pond snail

Forceps

Dish containing pond water

Lettuce leaf section

Paper towel

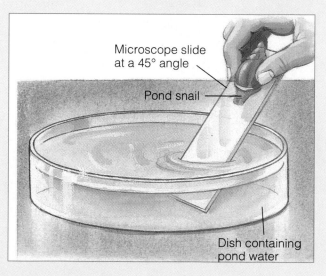

Microscope slide at a 45° angle

Pond snail

Dish containing pond water

Observations

1. How much of each food was eaten? Is the snail a carnivore or a herbivore?

2. How long did it take the pond snail to travel down the microscope slide? To travel up the slide?

3. How long did it take the pond snail to travel down the microscope slide covered with sandpaper? To travel up the slide?

Analysis and Conclusions

1. What is the pond snail's favorite food? How were you able to determine this?

2. Do snails travel up and down at the same rate? If not, what do you think accounts for the difference?

3. Share your results with your classmates. Were the results similar? Were they different? If they were different, explain why.

4. How does the texture of a surface affect the pond snail's speed?

Going Further

You may wish to repeat steps 5 through 7 in the activity using other materials to cover the microscope slide. Determine how fast the snail can travel over the surfaces of these materials.

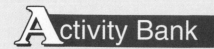

OFF AND RUNNING

Sow bugs are also called pill bugs because when disturbed they curl up into a tight, round pill shape. Pill bugs, which are really crustaceans and not insects, hibernate in the winter. However, they can be found under rocks or under piles of dead leaves close to the foundation of a house. To find out more about pill bugs, hold a pill bug derby. All you will need is a pencil, a sheet of unlined white paper, a pill bug, a clock with a second indicator, and a metric ruler.

What Do You Need to Do?

Have each member of the class use a pencil to mark an X in the middle of a sheet of unlined white paper. One member of your class should act as the official timer. When the timer shouts "Go!" each person should place their pill bug on the X and let it go. The timer should clock one minute while you track your racer with a pencil line. When the minute is up, measure the distance of your racer's trail. The pill bug that travels the farthest is the winner. On your mark, get ready, go!

What Did You Discover?

1. How many legs do pill bugs have?
2. Describe the other characteristics of pill bugs.
3. Based on the above information, to what group of animals do pill bugs belong?
4. Share with your classmates the distance your pill bug traveled. What was the greatest distance a pill bug traveled? The least distance?

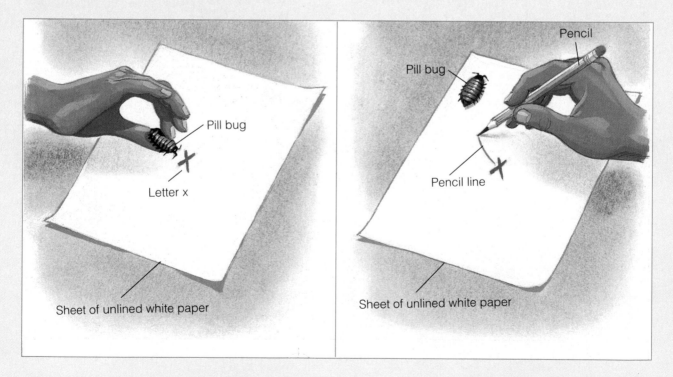

SPINNING WEBS

Do all spiders produce silk? Yes, they do. Some spiders, however, do not use the silk to build webs. Those spiders that do use silk to build webs weave intricate patterns. To see how a spider goes about spinning its web, or nest, perform this activity.

What You Will Need

wire coat hanger
wood block (10 cm x 40 cm x 1 cm)
large, clear plastic bag with twist tie
black-and-yellow garden spider

What You Will Do

1. Remove the hooked part of a wire coat hanger by bending it back and forth a few times.

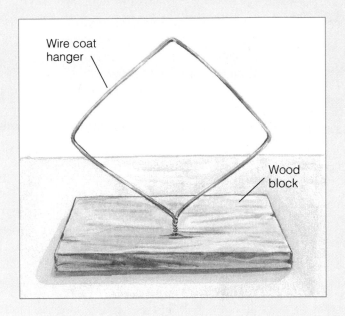

2. Bend the coat hanger into the shape of a square. Then insert the hanger, sharp side down, into a wood block so that it is supported by the wood block as shown in the drawing. This is called a net frame.

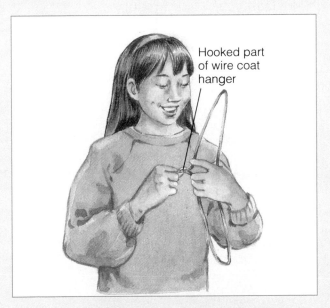

3. Blow up a large plastic bag and put the net frame inside.

4. Quickly place a black-and-yellow garden spider on the wood block and seal the plastic bag with the twist tie.

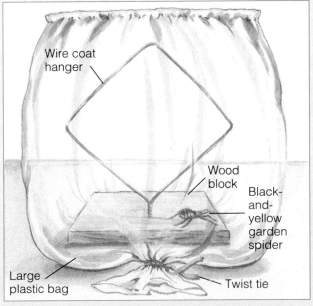

(continued)

5. Place the net frame in a place where it will remain undisturbed for two days. Record your daily observations in a data table similar to the one shown.

What You Will See

DATA TABLE

Day	Observations
1	
2	

What You Will Discover

1. Did your spider weave a web?
2. What time of day did your spider start to weave its web?
3. Did your spider build just one web?
4. Did your spider rebuild its web or did it build a new web?
5. If your spider built a new web, how often did it do so?
6. Share your results with your classmates. Were their results similiar? Different? Can you explain why?

Going Further

Release flying insects such as fruit flies and regular flies into the plastic bag with your spider. What happens to the insects? How does your spider react?

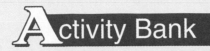

HOW MANY ARE TOO MANY?

In nature, there is a maximum size of a population that a particular environment can support at any one time. This is known as the carrying capacity. To actually determine the carrying capacity of a population of fruit flies, why not try this activity.

What You Will Need

culture bottle of fruit flies
sheet of unlined white paper
pencil
small paintbrush

What You Must Do

1. Carefully examine a culture bottle of fruit flies to identify their basic needs of life.

2. Count the number of fruit flies in the culture bottle. You might find it easier to count the fruit flies when they are inactive. To make the flies inactive, place the bottle of fruit flies in a freezer for one to two minutes. The cold temperature will slow them down.

3. Remove the plug from the culture bottle. Gently shake the fruit flies onto a sheet of unlined white paper and count them. As soon as you see the flies becoming active again, brush them back into the bottle and refrigerate them again, if you need to.

4. Count the number of fruit flies every two days for two weeks. Record this information in a data table similar to the one shown on the next page.

Culture bottle of fruit flies

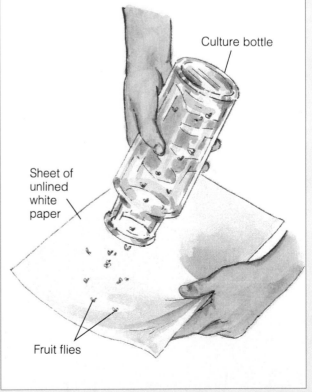

Culture bottle

Sheet of unlined white paper

Fruit flies

(continued)

What You Will See

DATA TABLE

Day	Number of Fruit Flies
1	
2	
3	
4	

What You Will Discover

1. What are the four basic needs of life?

2. Which of the four basic needs of life are limited in this activity? Which are unlimited? Explain.

3. What changes did you see in the population of fruit flies?

Going Further

Do you think the information from this activity can be applied to changes in the human population of the world? Explain your answer.

TO FLOAT OR NOT TO FLOAT?

How are most fishes able to swim at various depths in water? Bony fishes can raise or lower themselves in the water by adding gases to or removing them from their swim bladders. A swim bladder is a gas-filled chamber that adjusts the buoyancy of the fish to the water pressure at various depths. Water pressure is the force that water exerts over a certain area due to its weight and motion. To see firsthand how a swim bladder works, try this activity.

Materials

medicine dropper
2-L clear plastic soft drink bottle with cap

Procedure

1. Select one member of your group to act as the Principal Investigator and another to act as the Recorder. The other members of the group will be the Observers.
2. Fill the plastic soft drink bottle to the very top with water.

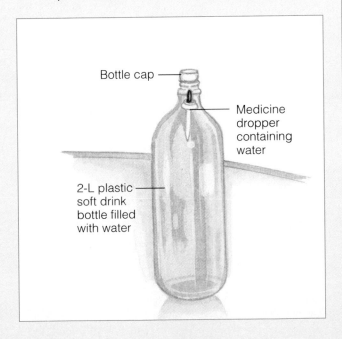

Bottle cap

Medicine dropper containing water

2-L plastic soft drink bottle filled with water

3. Place the medicine dropper in the bottle of water. The water should overflow. You may have to draw in or squeeze out more water from the medicine dropper so that it barely floats.
4. Screw the cap tightly on the plastic bottle. No water or air should leak out when the bottle is squeezed.

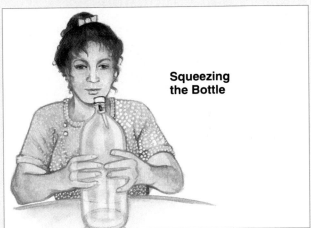

Squeezing the Bottle

Releasing the Bottle

5. Squeeze the sides of the bottle. Notice what happens.
6. Release the sides of the bottle. Notice what happens.
7. Have the Investigator and the Recorder reverse roles and repeat steps 5 and 6.

(continued)

Observations

1. What happens to the medicine dropper when the sides of the bottle are squeezed?

2. What happens to the medicine dropper when the sides of the bottle are released?

Analysis and Conclusions

1. What happens to the pressure of the water when you squeeze the sides of the plastic bottle?

2. Why is some of the water pushed up into the medicine dropper when you squeeze the bottle?

3. Why does the medicine dropper sink when you squeeze the sides of the bottle?

4. Why does the medicine dropper rise when you release the sides of the plastic bottle?

5. Two fishes are very similar in size to each other. However, one has more mass than the other. Which fish has more buoyancy?

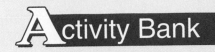
DO OIL AND WATER MIX?

An oil spill is an environmental disaster. Not only can an oil spill be fatal to ocean life but it can also endanger sea birds by damaging their feathers. To find out the effect of water and oil on the feathers of birds, try this activity.

Materials

hand lens
natural bird feather
small container of water
medicine dropper
small container of cooking oil

Procedure

1. Select one member of your group to be the Principal Investigator and another member to act as the Timer. The remaining members of the group will be the Observers.

2. With the hand lens, examine a natural bird feather.

3. Dip the feather into water for 1 minute. Take the feather out of the water and examine it with the hand lens.

4. Dip the feather into the cooking oil for 1 minute. Take it out and examine it with the hand lens.

5. Now dip the oil-covered feather back into the water for 1 minute. Take it out and examine it with the hand lens.

Observations

Describe the appearance of the feather in steps 2 through 5.

Analysis and Conclusions

1. What are the major changes in the feather after being placed in water? After being placed in oil?

2. What happened to the oil-covered feather when it was dipped in water?

3. How does exposure to oil affect normal bird activities?

4. What are some other examples of human-caused pollutants that can have harmful effects on wildlife?

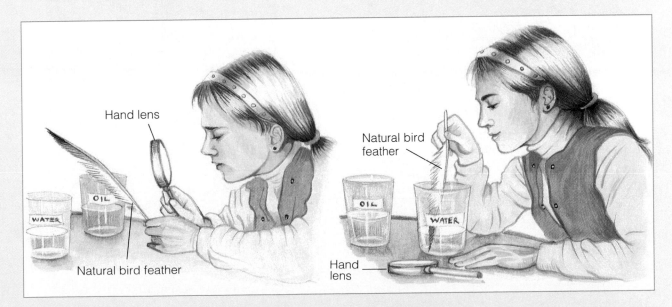

Hand lens

Natural bird feather

Natural bird feather

Hand lens

AN EGGS-AGGERATION

Can you remove the shell from a hard-boiled egg without cracking it? The shell of an egg is made of a substance called calcium carbonate. Calcium carbonate will dissolve in vinegar (acetic acid) to form a solution. Why not try your hand at this activity and see if you can remove the shell without cracking it. You will need a cold hard-boiled egg, a wide-mouthed jar, some vinegar, safety goggles, and tongs.

What You Will Do 🧪 🧰

1. Place a cold hard-boiled egg in a wide-mouthed jar.

2. Add enough vinegar to cover the egg.

3. Put the jar in a place where it will remain undisturbed overnight.

4. The next morning remove the egg with tongs. Observe the egg.

What You Will See

Describe what happened to the egg.

What You Will Discover

1. What happened to the shell? Did it disappear completely?

2. What do you think happened to the shell?

STRICTLY FOR THE BIRDS

Have you ever tried to make a bird's nest? It is not as easy as you may think. Why not try this activity and discover for yourself.

What You Will Do

1. Collect some straw from a field or from along the edges of your yard where the grass has not been mowed.
2. With scissors, cut a handful of straw or grass.
3. Now turn the handful of straw around and around in your hand as shown in the diagram on the left.

4. Try to form the straw into a donut shape using your thumbs to hollow out the middle as shown in the diagram on the right.

What You Will Discover

1. Is your nest very strong?
2. Drop it on a table. Does your nest stay together?
3. Who can make a better bird's nest—you or a bird? Why do you think this is true?
4. What other materials do birds use in making a nest?

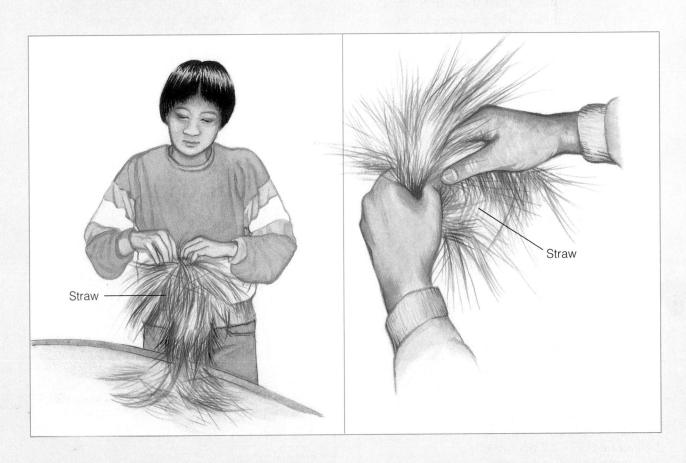

Straw

Straw

$\mathbf{A}$ppendix A

The metric system of measurement is used by scientists throughout the world. It is based on units of ten. Each unit is ten times larger or ten times smaller than the next unit. The most commonly used units of the metric system are given below. After you have finished reading about the metric system, try to put it to use. How tall are you in metrics? What is your mass? What is your normal body temperature in degrees Celsius?

Commonly Used Metric Units

Length   The distance from one point to another

meter (m)   A meter is slightly longer than a yard.
             1 meter = 1000 millimeters (mm)
             1 meter = 100 centimeters (cm)
             1000 meters = 1 kilometer (km)

Volume   The amount of space an object takes up

liter (L)   A liter is slightly more than a quart.
             1 liter = 1000 milliliters (mL)

Mass   The amount of matter in an object

gram (g)   A gram has a mass equal to about
            one paper clip.

            1000 grams = 1 kilogram (kg)

Temperature   The measure of hotness or coldness

degrees   0°C = freezing point of water
Celsius (°C) 100°C = boiling point of water

Metric–English Equivalents

2.54 centimeters (cm) = 1 inch (in.)
1 meter (m) = 39.37 inches (in.)
1 kilometer (km) = 0.62 miles (mi)
1 liter (L) = 1.06 quarts (qt)
250 milliliters (mL) = 1 cup (c)
1 kilogram (kg) = 2.2 pounds (lb)
28.3 grams (g) = 1 ounce (oz)
$°C = 5/9 \times (°F - 32)$

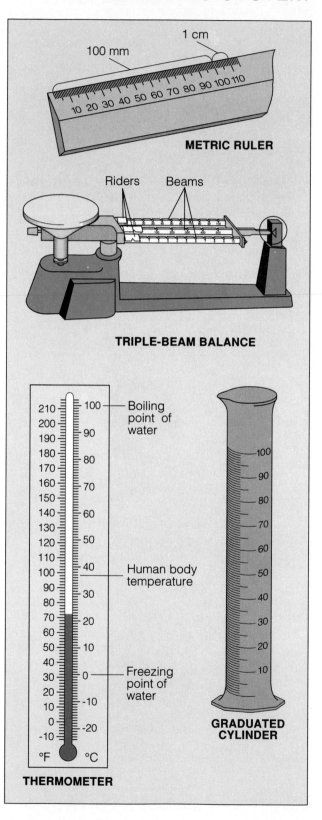

METRIC RULER

TRIPLE-BEAM BALANCE

THERMOMETER

GRADUATED CYLINDER

Glassware Safety

1. Whenever you see this symbol, you will know that you are working with glassware that can easily be broken. Take particular care to handle such glassware safely. And never use broken or chipped glassware.
2. Never heat glassware that is not thoroughly dry. Never pick up any glassware unless you are sure it is not hot. If it is hot, use heat-resistant gloves.
3. Always clean glassware thoroughly before putting it away.

Fire Safety

1. Whenever you see this symbol, you will know that you are working with fire. Never use any source of fire without wearing safety goggles.
2. Never heat anything—particularly chemicals—unless instructed to do so.
3. Never heat anything in a closed container.
4. Never reach across a flame.
5. Always use a clamp, tongs, or heat-resistant gloves to handle hot objects.
6. Always maintain a clean work area, particularly when using a flame.

Heat Safety

Whenever you see this symbol, you will know that you should put on heat-resistant gloves to avoid burning your hands.

Chemical Safety

1. Whenever you see this symbol, you will know that you are working with chemicals that could be hazardous.
2. Never smell any chemical directly from its container. Always use your hand to waft some of the odors from the top of the container toward your nose—and only when instructed to do so.
3. Never mix chemicals unless instructed to do so.
4. Never touch or taste any chemical unless instructed to do so.
5. Keep all lids closed when chemicals are not in use. Dispose of all chemicals as instructed by your teacher.

6. Immediately rinse with water any chemicals, particularly acids, that get on your skin and clothes. Then notify your teacher.

Eye and Face Safety

1. Whenever you see this symbol, you will know that you are performing an experiment in which you must take precautions to protect your eyes and face by wearing safety goggles.
2. When you are heating a test tube or bottle, always point it away from you and others. Chemicals can splash or boil out of a heated test tube.

Sharp Instrument Safety

1. Whenever you see this symbol, you will know that you are working with a sharp instrument.
2. Always use single-edged razors; double-edged razors are too dangerous.
3. Handle any sharp instrument with extreme care. Never cut any material toward you; always cut away from you.
4. Immediately notify your teacher if your skin is cut.

Electrical Safety

1. Whenever you see this symbol, you will know that you are using electricity in the laboratory.
2. Never use long extension cords to plug in any electrical device. Do not plug too many appliances into one socket or you may overload the socket and cause a fire.
3. Never touch an electrical appliance or outlet with wet hands.

Animal Safety

1. Whenever you see this symbol, you will know that you are working with live animals.
2. Do not cause pain, discomfort, or injury to an animal.
3. Follow your teacher's directions when handling animals. Wash your hands thoroughly after handling animals or their cages.

One of the first things a scientist learns is that working in the laboratory can be an exciting experience. But the laboratory can also be quite dangerous if proper safety rules are not followed at all times. To prepare yourself for a safe year in the laboratory, read over the following safety rules. Then read them a second time. Make sure you understand each rule. If you do not, ask your teacher to explain any rules you are unsure of.

Dress Code

1. Many materials in the laboratory can cause eye injury. To protect yourself from possible injury, wear safety goggles whenever you are working with chemicals, burners, or any substance that might get into your eyes. Never wear contact lenses in the laboratory.

2. Wear a laboratory apron or coat whenever you are working with chemicals or heated substances.

3. Tie back long hair to keep it away from any chemicals, burners and candles, or other laboratory equipment.

4. Remove or tie back any article of clothing or jewelry that can hang down and touch chemicals and flames.

General Safety Rules

5. Read all directions for an experiment several times. Follow the directions exactly as they are written. If you are in doubt about any part of the experiment, ask your teacher for assistance.

6. Never perform activities that are not authorized by your teacher. Obtain permission before "experimenting" on your own.

7. Never handle any equipment unless you have specific permission.

8. Take extreme care not to spill any material in the laboratory. If a spill occurs, immediately ask your teacher about the proper cleanup procedure. Never simply pour chemicals or other substances into the sink or trash container.

9. Never eat in the laboratory.

10. Wash your hands before and after each experiment.

First Aid

11. Immediately report all accidents, no matter how minor, to your teacher.

12. Learn what to do in case of specific accidents, such as getting acid in your eyes or on your skin. (Rinse acids from your body with lots of water.)

13. Become aware of the location of the first-aid kit. But your teacher should administer any required first aid due to injury. Or your teacher may send you to the school nurse or call a physician.

14. Know where and how to report an accident or fire. Find out the location of the fire extinguisher, phone, and fire alarm. Keep a list of important phone numbers—such as the fire department and the school nurse—near the phone. Immediately report any fires to your teacher.

Heating and Fire Safety

15. Again, never use a heat source, such as a candle or burner, without wearing safety goggles.

16. Never heat a chemical you are not instructed to heat. A chemical that is harmless when cool may be dangerous when heated.

17. Maintain a clean work area and keep all materials away from flames.

18. Never reach across a flame.

19. Make sure you know how to light a Bunsen burner. (Your teacher will demonstrate the proper procedure for lighting a burner.) If the flame leaps out of a burner toward you, immediately turn off the gas. Do not touch the burner. It may be hot. And never leave a lighted burner unattended!

20. When heating a test tube or bottle, always point it away from you and others. Chemicals can splash or boil out of a heated test tube.

21. Never heat a liquid in a closed container. The expanding gases produced may blow the container apart, injuring you or others.

22. Before picking up a container that has been heated, first hold the back of your hand near it. If you can feel the heat on the back of your hand, the container may be too hot to handle. Use a clamp or tongs when handling hot containers.

Using Chemicals Safely

23. Never mix chemicals for the "fun of it." You might produce a dangerous, possibly explosive substance.

24. Never touch, taste, or smell a chemical unless you are instructed by your teacher to do so. Many chemicals are poisonous. If you are instructed to note the fumes in an experiment, gently wave your hand over the opening of a container and direct the fumes toward your nose. Do not inhale the fumes directly from the container.

25. Use only those chemicals needed in the activity. Keep all lids closed when a chemical is not being used. Notify your teacher whenever chemicals are spilled.

26. Dispose of all chemicals as instructed by your teacher. To avoid contamination, never return chemicals to their original containers.

27. Be extra careful when working with acids or bases. Pour such chemicals over the sink, not over your workbench.

28. When diluting an acid, pour the acid into water. Never pour water into an acid.

29. Immediately rinse with water any acids that get on your skin or clothing. Then notify your teacher of any acid spill.

Using Glassware Safely

30. Never force glass tubing into a rubber stopper. A turning motion and lubricant will be helpful when inserting glass tubing into rubber stoppers or rubber tubing. Your teacher will demonstrate the proper way to insert glass tubing.

31. Never heat glassware that is not thoroughly dry. Use a wire screen to protect glassware from any flame.

32. Keep in mind that hot glassware will not appear hot. Never pick up glassware without first checking to see if it is hot. See #22.

33. If you are instructed to cut glass tubing, fire-polish the ends immediately to remove sharp edges.

34. Never use broken or chipped glassware. If glassware breaks, notify your teacher and dispose of the glassware in the proper trash container.

35. Never eat or drink from laboratory glassware. Thoroughly clean glassware before putting it away.

Using Sharp Instruments

36. Handle scalpels or razor blades with extreme care. Never cut material toward you; cut away from you.

37. Immediately notify your teacher if you cut your skin when working in the laboratory.

Animal Safety

38. No experiments that will cause pain, discomfort, or harm to mammals, birds, reptiles, fishes, and amphibians should be done in the classroom or at home.

39. Animals should be handled only if necessary. If an animal is excited or frightened, pregnant, feeding, or with its young, special handling is required.

40. Your teacher will instruct you as to how to handle each animal species that may be brought into the classroom.

41. Clean your hands thoroughly after handling animals or the cage containing animals.

End-of-Experiment Rules

42. After an experiment has been completed, clean up your work area and return all equipment to its proper place.

43. Wash your hands after every experiment.

44. Turn off all burners before leaving the laboratory. Check that the gas line leading to the burner is off as well.

Glossary

Pronunciation Key

When difficult names or terms first appear in the text, they are respelled to aid pronunciation. A syllable in SMALL CAPITAL LETTERS receives the most stress. The key below lists the letters used for respelling. It includes examples of words using each sound and shows how the words would be respelled.

Symbol	Example	Respelling
a	hat	(hat)
ay	pay, late	(pay), (layt)
ah	star, hot	(stahr), (haht)
ai	air, dare	(air), (dair)
aw	law, all	(law), (awl)
eh	met	(meht)
ee	bee, eat	(bee), (eet)
er	learn, sir, fur	(lern), (ser), (fer)
ih	fit	(fiht)
igh	mile, sigh	(mighl), (sigh)
oh	no	(noh)
oi	soil, boy	(soil), (boi)
oo	root, rule	(root), (rool)
or	born, door	(born), (dor)
ow	plow, out	(plow), (owt)

Symbol	Example	Respelling
u	put, book	(put), (buk)
uh	fun	(fuhn)
yoo	few, use	(fyoo), (yooz)
ch	chill, reach	(chihl), (reech)
g	go, dig	(goh), (dihg)
j	jet, gently, bridge	(jeht), (JEHNTlee), (brihj)
k	kite, cup	(kight), (kuhp)
ks	mix	(mihks)
kw	quick	(kwihk)
ng	bring	(brihng)
s	say, cent	(say), (sehnt)
sh	she, crash	(shee), (krash)
th	three	(three)
y	yet, onion	(yeht), (UHN yuhn)
z	zip, always	(zihp), (AWL wayz)
zh	treasure	(TREH zher)

asexual reproduction: process by which a single organism produces a new organism

autotroph (AW-toh-trahf): organism that can make its own food

coldblooded: having a body temperature that changes somewhat with the temperature of the surroundings

contour feather: largest and most familiar feather that gives birds their streamlined shape

down: short, fluffy feather that acts as insulation

egg-laying mammal: warmblooded vertebrate with hair or fur that lays eggs; monotreme

external fertilization: process in which a sperm joins with an egg outside the body

exoskeleton: rigid outer covering in most arthropods

feather: important characteristic of birds; helps to insulate the body and is used in flying

gestation (jehs-TAY-shuhn) **period:** time the young of placental mammals spend inside the mother

gill: feathery structure through which water-dwelling animals breathe

heterotroph (HEHT-er-oh-trahf): organism that cannot make its own food

host: organism upon which another organism lives

internal fertilization: process in which a sperm joins with an egg inside the body

invertebrate: animal that has no backbone

kingdom: large general classification group

larva (LAHR-vuh): second stage in metamorphosis, when an egg hatches

metamorphosis (meht-uh-MOR-fuh-sihs): process by which an organism undergoes dramatic changes in body form in its life cycle

migrate: to move to a new environment during the course of a year

molting: process by which an arthropod's exoskeleton is shed and replaced from time to time

nematocyst (NEHM-uh-toh-sihst): stinging structure used by a cnidarian to stun or kill its prey

parasite: organism that grows on or in other living organisms

pheromone (FER-uh-mohn): powerful chemical given off by an insect to attract a mate

placenta (pluh-SEHN-tuh): structure that develops in pregnant female placental mammals through which food, oxygen, and wastes are exchanged between young and mother

placental (pluh-SEHN-tuhl) **mammal:** warmblooded vertebrate with hair or fur that gives birth to young that have remained inside the mother's body until their body systems are able to function independently

pouched mammal: warmblooded vertebrate with hair or fur that gives birth to young that are not well developed; marsupial

pupa (PYOO-puh): third stage in the metamorphosis of an insect

regeneration: ability to regrow lost parts

sexual reproduction: process by which a new organism forms from the joining of a female cell and a male cell

spicule (SPIHK-yool): thin, spiny structure that forms the skeleton of many sponges

swim bladder: gas-filled sac that gives bony fishes buoyancy

territory: area where an individual animal lives

tube foot: suction-cuplike structure connected to the water vascular system of an echinoderm

vertebrate: animal that has a backbone, or vertebral column

warmblooded: having a body temperature that stays constant

water vascular system: fluid-filled internal tubes that carry food and oxygen, remove wastes, and help echinoderms move

Index

176 ■ C